MW00658171

Dream—I Dare You

Julia Gentry

UNINHIBITED
PUBLISHING

DENVER

Dream—I Dare You: A Wake-Up Call to Create Greater Alignment in Your
Faith, Family, Career, and Community
Published by Uninhibited Publishing
Denver, CO

Copyright ©2021 by Julia Gentry All rights reserved.

No part of this book may be reproduced in any form or by any mechanical means, including information
storage and retrieval systems without permission in writing from the publisher/author, except by a reviewer
who may quote passages in a review.

All images, logos, quotes, and trademarks included in this book are subject to use according to trademark
and copyright laws of the United States of America.

All Bible verses are taken from the New International Version (NIV) unless otherwise noted. The Holy
Bible, New International Version® NIV® Copyright © 1973, 1978, 1984, 2011 by Biblica, Inc.TM Used by
permission. All rights reserved worldwide.

Bible verses marked (MSG) are taken from *THE MESSAGE*, copyright © 1993, 2002, 2018 by Eugene H.
Peterson. Used by permission of NavPress. All rights reserved. Represented by Tyndale House Publishers, Inc.

Bible verses marked (NLT) are taken from the Holy Bible, New Living Translation, copyright ©1996, 2004,
2015 by Tyndale House Foundation. Used by permission of Tyndale House Publishers, Carol Stream, Illinois
60188. All rights reserved.

Bible verses marked Christian Standard Bible are taken from The Christian Standard Bible. Copyright ©
2017 by Holman Bible Publishers. Used by permission. Christian Standard Bible®, and CSB® are federally
registered trademarks of Holman Bible Publishers, all rights reserved.

Bible verses marked World English Bible are taken from the World English Bible® version. Public Domain.

Bible verses marked (KJV) are taken from the King James Version. Public Domain.

Bible verses marked American Standard Version are taken from the American Standard Version.
Public Domain.

ISBN: 978-1-7357859-0-5
SELF-HELP / Spiritual

Interior design by Victoria Wolf, wolfdesignandmarketing.com. Cover art by Maria Barry

QUANTITY PURCHASES: Schools, companies, professional groups, clubs, and other organizations
may qualify for special terms when ordering quantities of this title. For information, email
julia@thedreamfactoryandco.com

All rights reserved by Julia Gentry and Uninhibited Publishing.
Printed in the United States of America.

UNINHIBITED
PUBLISHING

God,

You gave me the gift of life.

The least I could do is give you this book in return.

-Me

Contents

SECTION 2: Building Your Belief

SECTION 3: Living to Create

Before You
BLOW YOUR MIND...

THIS BOOK IS DESIGNED to transform you. It's designed to grow you, to give you the space to become the person you were created to be. It is not for you to rush through it. It is not a quick read. It's likely to blow your mind, allowing you to become *wholehearted* in your approach. It's intended for you to take it chapter by chapter, piece by piece, and work on yourself from the inside out, so you not only clarify your dreams but also *obtain* and *sustain* them.

With that being said, here's a quick down and dirty on how to use this book to maximize your dreaming process.

First things first, this book is written in three sections which is parallel to my growth coaching model:

1. Creating Awareness
2. Building Belief
3. Taking Action

Section 1: Creating Awareness is just as it implies. It's 100 percent designed to give you the tools in your toolbox to support you as you become aware. Believe it or not, there are reasons for our lack of awareness, one of which is because it's flat-out hard. It's hard to rethink, hard to dream (especially if you've never done so before), hard to break patterns, and it's hard to look at your past for the sake of your future. Yet, it's all par for the course if you want to create change in the world around you. These first four chapters are designed to give you everything you need to know as you start to *know*. Consider these the most important tools in your toolbox as you build your house called life.

Section 2: Building Belief is designed to help you build a solid foundation of truth on which to build your dreams and your life. Getting to the truth means we have to wade through the waters of lies. We have to re-establish thought patterns and habits. It's a willingness to look at things for what they are while also having the courage to imagine what they could be. This section contains the meatiest chapters of the book and is also the most transformational *when applied*. It is very interactive and requires you to lean in and respond.

Section 3: Living to Create is designed to get you moving toward the fulfillment of your dreams. A dream with no plan of action is no dream at all. The last two chapters are created to support you in becoming your own activist, to give you the confidence to do something with the dreams you hold within, and to provide insight into the mindset and tactics to approach each day heart forward and mind right. Like Section 2, it is very interactive and needs your participation to get the biggest bang for your buck. The exercises within this are not rhetorical, so I encourage you to *do* the work.

Along with this book, I have also created companion pieces, **DREAM: Workbook** and **DREAM: Journal**. These are intended to *amplify* your dreaming process but aren't required. The workbook supports you in exploring each chapter and exercise without the five-line minimum I allow in this book. The journal gives you even more space, uninhibited and without limits, to hear your heart speak. Please keep in mind that I do purposefully give space to write directly in this book, so in and of itself, it's designed to do the job!

Bottom line, my greatest intentions for you as you read this book are threefold:

RETHINK! Dreamers think differently; they have to. This book is designed to support you in that process, to help you rethink anything and everything so you can get different results.

AWAKEN AND ALIGN! I am on a mission to create a massive wake-up call that ignites people, outside the four walls of the church, to be the light in the dark and the salt of the earth, to remind us that we are called to be bold as lions in our faith, family, career, and community. We need to live awake. So make no bones about it, this book is designed to wake you up. It's also designed to align you with the truth. In order to be the light of the world, we need to be aligned with God and what heaven's doing. We need to be about *His* business, connected with Him, in flow with what He's doing, and dreaming what He's dreaming, so we can do our part to bring heaven to this earth.

MOBILIZE! "Faith by itself, if it is not accompanied by action, is dead" (James 2:17). Dreaming without the fulfillment of those dreams is no dream at all. This book is meant to get you to take action, to *do* something with the things God's given you to do. If not you, who?

This book will cause you to grow.

And let's be honest, growing is hard because it challenges the status quo, pushes the envelope, and takes you outside your comfort zone. But not growing is also hard. Playing small, settling for status quo, and not reaching your fullest potential is also hard.

It's time to *pick your hard*.

It's time to dream.

DREAM ON.

DEDICATION

THIS BOOK IS DEDICATED to Malori Aslan Smith.

My best friend Malori died when she was seventeen years old on June 30, 2002, while on a mission trip in Mexico. I was just sixteen. At the time of writing this book, she has been gone as long as she was alive.

Though it feels like forever ago and yesterday all at the same time, I can still remember receiving the fateful news and falling to the floor, thinking I'd never have the strength to get up again. I can remember questioning *everything* about this life. I questioned everything about God. I can remember questioning everything about friendship. I can remember feeling this intense void and a literal pain in my stomach.

And yet, somehow, I got up, only my life was never the same again.

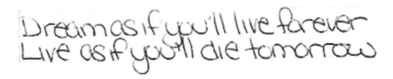

"Dream as if you'll live forever and live as if you'll die tomorrow" was one of Mal's last journal entries. She wrote it as if she knew something. Little did I know that it would become a resounding sound in my ears and the unapologetic cry of my heart.

If I'm honest, it's taken me a long time to dream, for many reasons, all of which I will share in the pages that follow, but I can finally honestly say that because of dreaming and the process God has walked me through, I have gotten my life back. So Malori, thank you for the gift you gave me with your life and even in your death.

I also dedicate this book to my kids. I pray that beyond the words on these pages, the life I choose to live is one that shows you the only way to live is to chase your dreams heart first, all out, all in, and completely unapologetic. To all four of you, my greatest dreams come true, Malachi, Aslan, Nixon, and Zion, I hope you know how much I adore you and that along with my own dreams, I will also live my life chasing *any* dream you have too!

I dedicate this book to my husband, Travis Gentry. More than anyone else in my lifetime, you've given me the space and the beautiful chance to dream, and there is no one, *no one*, I'd rather dream with than you. Somewhere between the line of brilliant and insane is where you've inspired me to live my life. I aspire to be someone who keeps you running toward every dream you ever have, as you do the same for me. And I hope just once that I'm fast enough to beat you to the top!

And last but not least, this is dedicated to all my dreamers out there. Even as I write this, tears run down my face, partially because I still miss Malori so much and partially because with everything I am on the inside of me, I want all of us to dream, every single one of us—including *you*. Whoever you are, wherever you come from, no matter how bad your past has been or how bleak your future may seem, no matter how old or young you are, and no matter how many successes or failures you've experienced, dreaming is your right. It's one of the greatest blessings this life can offer us, and it's yours for the taking *if* you reach out and grab it.

You might be thinking:

I don't know how.

You don't know my past.

You don't know what's happened to me.

You don't know what I have working against me.

You're right. I don't. But here's one thing I *do* know— you're still alive. You're here, on this planet, breathing, which is one luxury Malori and those who have gone before us don't have, and because you're still here, it tells me you've got purpose, meaning, choice, and most importantly, the opportunity to dream. Take it, run with it, and make all those who have gone before us proud.

Heaven and all our angels are watching and cheering us on.

I am honored and psyched that you picked up this book, not for my benefit but for your own. May you *never* convince yourself that life isn't 100 percent about dreaming. May you *never* convince yourself that you need to grow up or "get real." May you *never* convince yourself that it's too risky to live the life of your dreams. May you commit your life to dreaming and chasing those dreams that are on the inside of you. And may you know that you have a life-long advocate and a real fan in me.

With my *whole* heart,

INTRODUCTION

Why Did I Write This Book?

"For the creation waits in eager expectation for the children of God to be revealed" (Romans 8:19).

"But the righteous are as bold as a lion" (Proverbs 28:1).

What does dreaming have to do with life?

Well, everything.

The push to write this book began back in January of 2018 after my husband and I decided to pursue a lifelong dream to travel the country in an RV. Along with our three kids, all under the age of five, we sold just about everything we owned and set out on an adventure of a lifetime. It was also at the beginning of my own "midlife awakening." I was just shy of thirty years old and had built a successful company in real estate (which bought and sold millions of dollars' worth of real estate), only to be left with $100,000 of debt because I didn't have the tools that I am about to teach you in this book. From there, I rebuilt my career as a business coach, advising hundreds of business owners on how to build a successful company with plenty of insights into my own successes and epic failures. I bought the house and nice cars, had a few babies, obtained "the American Dream" only to realize it wasn't my dream, and every night as I crawled into bed, I still had this nagging question in the back of my mind: *Is there something more?*

Please note: if you have ever found yourself asking that question, then you, my friend, are a dreamer in waiting, a dreamer who is ready to wake up!

Well, right around six months into our full-time travel, we found ourselves parked in Phoenix, Arizona. This was after we had seen a good part of the country, from the majestic Grand Tetons in Wyoming to the stunning views of Horseshoe Bend in Arizona; the heaven on earth we found in Bend, Oregon to the creative town of Austin, Texas; from the snowy city of Park City, Utah to the insurmountable trees in the Redwood Forest in California. It was all truly amazing. On this particular night, it was a warm evening, the kids were all fast asleep, my husband was too, and I had just gotten done watching *The Greatest Showman*, a movie that I swear changed my life. I can remember slowly dozing off to sleep for what seemed to be only a few minutes but was actually a few hours. This was when it all started for me.

I had this dream where I had a bird's-eye view of people everywhere, all walks of life, ages, races, and varying lifestyles, who were each walking around, dead asleep to their lives. It was as if they were alive but not really living. They were physically present but not awake. They looked as if they were walking around like the Bergens out of a scene from the movie *Trolls*. Each appeared to be disheartened, numb, hopeless, reactive, unaware, and almost with this glassy-eyed look on their faces like they were there, but "no one was home." As I watched from my bird's-eye viewpoint, trying to figure out what caused such unaware, sad people, all of a sudden, I saw hundreds of shooting stars light up the dark sky, soaring overhead as though they had somewhere to be. I saw beautiful fire colors—red, orange, and yellow—it was magnificent and powerful. As I watched with amazement, the stars painted a word across the sky that read: *Dream*. With the power of that one word, every single person in my dream, who was asleep, started to wake up to their life.

Immediately I woke up.

I literally shot out of bed, completely out of breath, looking around in a total daze. I felt discombobulated because the dream had felt so real. But there I was, in Phoenix, Arizona, in my RV, with what felt like pure insights into the algorithm for life. *But how do I apply what I just saw? What does this mean? Why were people asleep to their lives? And why the word dream?* I thought, *DREAM? Really? Get real, Julia.*

I'm not going to lie; I felt a little embarrassed with the "out there" nature this dream suggested, and, therefore, I chalked it up as a *Greatest Showman* hangover (because those are real you know). I decided not to put a whole lot of extra thought into it and just let it lay on the pages of my heart.

Fast forward a few months; I'm having lunch with my mom back in Denver on a business trip, and I excuse myself to the ladies' room where an elderly woman greets me with a rather negative energy. We almost run into each other as I'm walking in and she's walking out, so I deem it only fair to greet her, "Hello, how are you?" I ask. And with a somewhat sarcastic response, she says, "Oh you know—living the dream." At first, I thought, that's awesome, you go girl, but then I realized that she didn't mean it in the way I had wished, and in fact, it was a very sarcastic response. I had to know more. I turned around and quickly asked, "May I ask, what's keeping you from actually living your dream?" Without batting an eye or turning around she said, "Life."

It crushed me. Here was this lady, at an age where she should absolutely be *living the dream,* and yet the sadness in her voice and the stillness in her soul was tangible. I thought, ***if life is stopping her from living the dream, what's the point of life?***

Perhaps it's not that life is really getting in the way of this lady living her dream, but maybe it's that she doesn't have a dream that's louder than her life to live for!

Bingo. And at that moment, my dream from the RV flashed before my eyes again.

Immediately I remembered that the moment the stars shot across the dark sky and the word *Dream* seemed to paint across the horizon, and everyone who was once asleep to their lives started waking up. They went from being completely asleep to their lives to awake, alive, aware, and in complete alignment. It was like looking at well-lit lighthouses up on a hill, shining ever so bright and full of life. Only I wasn't looking at lighthouses, I was looking at people. Awake people.

"We have to dream!" I said out loud. "If we want to wake up to our lives, we have to wake up to our dreams."

I was then drawn to a verse in the Bible that says, "In the last days, God says, I will pour out my Spirit on all the people. **Your sons and daughters will prophesy, your young men will see visions, your old men will dream dreams**. Even on my servants, both men and women, I will pour out my Spirit in those days, and they will prophesy. I will show wonders in the heavens above and signs on the earth below" (Acts 2:17–19 [emphasis mine]).

That's where this whole thing started for me. And if no one else is going to advocate for this, I will because I believe that now, more than ever before, we need people who are awake! We need a church, outside of its four walls, that is awake. We need *you*, awake.

More than ever before, our world needs you, me, and each one of us, awake, alert, and aligned. The world needs the very dreams God's put within us to manifest themselves in the world around us. For every problem we see today, for every heartache we're experiencing, for every injustice, wrongdoing, up-side-down system, He has created solutions—only those solutions don't lie dormant in the world around us. They lie dormant in the world within us. It is time for a massive wake-up call to ignite each and every one of us to be the light in the dark, the salt of the earth. It is time for us to be as bold as lions!

The book of Matthew says, "You are the salt of the earth but if the salt loses its saltiness, how can it be made salty again? It is no longer good for anything, except to be thrown out and trampled underfoot. You are the light of the world. A town on a hill cannot be hidden. Neither do people light a lamp and put it under a bowl. Instead, put it on a stand and it gives light to everyone in the house. In the same way, let your light shine before others, that they may see your good deeds and glorify your Father in heaven" (Matthew 5:13–16).

Are you a light to this world?

Are your deeds shining and actively pointing people to God?

Are you living "salty?"

If not you, who?

It *has* to start with you.

It has to start with *me*.

If not *us*, who?

"Everything is possible for one who believes" (Mark 9:23). Not some things. Not a few things. *Everything.* "Truly I tell you, if you have faith as small as a mustard seed, you can say to this mountain, 'Move from here to there,' and it will move. Nothing will be impossible for you" (Matthew 17:20).

Are you seeing these truths play out in your life? Are you seeing *everything* or *anything* play out in the world around you? Are you moving mountains with your faith? If not, why not?

Colossians 3 says, "So if you're serious about living this new resurrection life with Christ, act like it. Pursue the things over which Christ presides. Don't shuffle along, eyes to the ground, absorbed with the things right in front of you. Look up, and be alert to what is going on around Christ—that's where the action is. See things from his perspective… It wasn't long ago that you were doing all that stuff and not knowing any better. But you know better now." (Colossians 3:1–2, 7-8, The Message).

We know but do we *know?*

We see but do we *see?*

We hear but do we *hear?*

If we aren't manifesting His truth, it means we aren't connected to His truth. If we aren't actively demonstrating His power in all areas of life, then it means we are out of alignment. There is a disconnect, and we have to look at the root cause, which is exactly why I wrote this book, to create greater alignment. The greatest way we re-establish alignment is by dreaming. I wanted to give people just like you the chance to learn how to dream because in doing so, you can bridge the gap between what you currently have in life and what you want most, to turn any crisis (including a midlife crisis—no matter what age you are) into a midlife awakening that sets you free to live your life *consciously.* In dreaming, you wake up to your life, not only reconnecting with yourself but also with the voice of God *in* you. We do this by first doing what I call "going in," actually hearing ourselves and the God in us. Second, it's about "getting loud" by establishing vision, conviction, and an unapologetic approach to how we do life.

You see, dreaming isn't what most people think, which is why most people aren't getting as much out of life as they could. Dreaming is a game changer, and it's not for the faint of heart, but rather for those *of* heart. The Gallup organization, an American analytics and advisory company, says that 70 percent of people admit to being unfulfilled and dissatisfied in their life and work. That statistic is crazy to me, and its result is enormous squandered potential. This, among many other factors, is why I wrote this book. I literally lose sleep at night considering the devastation of that statistic.

Being a growth coach and working directly alongside hundreds and hundreds of individuals and entrepreneurs in the last decade, I have seen far too many people settle for "okay," "fine," and "good enough." I have seen people try to keep the peace around them only to start a war within themselves. I have seen far too many people justify their decisions in life based upon their past, upbringing, or current situation, which causes them to only relive their past versus create their future. I have seen far too many believers say they believe only to look like the rest of the world, in turn prohibiting the progress that's actually possible. And frankly, I have seen far too many people (Christians and not) blame God for things that He just didn't do. Here's what I know to be true: not conforming, truly believing, living life out of intention, in pursuit of your dreams and outside the status quo, trusting yourself, and fully trusting God can be hard, and it can also be lonely. Plus, it takes a certain type of mindset that has to be developed, refined, and supported. It takes courage to build something that's never been created, to do something that most people won't, to put your future on the line for something that is not guaranteed. But I believe there are people just like me who feel like they just can't *not* do it anymore and are willing to take the risk!

The key to getting our lives back on track to their truest, most awake and alive state is to simply get each one of us dreaming again, to get *you* dreaming again. I believe that the answer to most of the problems you're facing today will actually be solutions found on the inside, those deep, yet to be fulfilled dreams *if* what's on the inside of you comes out. But, the more you avoid those dreams, disregard them as nonsense, or come up with excuses and reasons not to pursue them, the further away you will be from the results you want most.

Many ask, "When is the best time to dream?" as though there is some opportune time to do so. There is no perfect time, the time is simply now. Anytime. All the time. Yesterday, today, tomorrow. It's never too late and you're never too early. That means, even in times of crisis, change, or when facing the unknown: it's time to dream. When you find yourself saying that life is just "okay," "fine," or "good enough": it's time to dream. When you feel stuck, bored, unmotivated, even depressed: it's time to dream. When you want to give up, feel defeated, feel behind the eight ball, and don't know where to start: it's time to dream. Especially when you find yourself asking: Is there something more? My answer to that question is always YES! It's time to dream!

I believe there is a song in you, a book waiting to be written, a business waiting to be launched, church doors waiting to be opened, an idea that needs to be heard, or a heart of courage just waiting to explode. Therefore, I couldn't *not* play my role in supporting those songs, books, ideas, businesses, churches, and hearts of courage waiting in the wings. I had to create this wake-up call for anyone who wants to manifest themselves and their dreams fully. And that's really what this book is. It's my own life's story of learning to become a dreamer and the questions I've cried over while I sat at the feet of God, coupled with my experience as a growth coach working with people just like you asking big, bold, deep questions about life. It is written in a way to not only open you up to you and the will of God for your life but to provide you with a tactical approach, so you get the most out of this wild journey we call life.

You see, I grew up in a very charismatic, Christian home. My parents divorced when I was five years old, and my mom dove head-first into the church. This was when her healing journey began. For me, it's all I knew. I saw the demonstration of God's power with my own eyes. I learned and could recite a ton of Bible verses from a very young age. But I admit, I was a product of knowing God but not *knowing* God, seeing but not *seeing*, believing but not *believing*. I have gone my own way. I have done my own thing. I have chased money, accomplishments, and all the stuff. I have spent thousands of dollars understanding how the mind, body, and brain work. I've studied energy, health, and nutrition and invested so much into my own understanding of business, entrepreneurship, and all the things. I get the power of How-Tos and have learned from some of the best experts in their field. AND. AND. It is empty without the demonstration and manifestation of who God really is, alive and working in and through me, He doing His part and me doing mine. ✳ Too often I see the world (non-believers) forfeit its understanding of God and who He is for willpower. This co-exist mentality, summarized with a bunch of universal truths, leave most feeling unfulfilled. Accomplished, sure. But unfulfilled, absolutely. Many know a lot at a cognitive level. We know a lot about money, science, the mind, body, health and nutrition, how to be successful in business, and how to achieve. The How-Tos are out there, so we Google more, yet we *know* less. Then we seek out professional advice and don't get me wrong, the behemoths of industries are exceptional in what they do, no doubt about it. Still, for many, as we begin to listen to them more, we listen to ourselves less and less. If we're not careful, we miss the real, demonstrated power of God, the manifestation of His holy presence working in and through us to do even greater things than we've already done or conceivably know how to do. For those of you who don't know God or are even a little skeptical as you read this, my hope is this book blows your mind and everything you thought you knew about God, so you can really *know* Him. I encourage you, in the pages to come, to rethink God. I did. And it's changed everything. All I ask is you have the courage to look at the weariness within you, the striving around you, and consider a piece to the equation you may be missing: God. ✳

Equally, I see the church forfeit its ability to be co-creators with God in this life. Too many of us know God's scripture at a head level, but it hasn't transformed who we are at a heart level. It hasn't changed our behavior. And I think it's because we haven't utilized the tools that have been developed in the world around us. It's like we are in a boat, ready to hit a cliff, praying that God will steer us away only to completely overlook the oars, motor, and sail that have been provided to us in our boat. We pray, and we pray, and we pray only to hit the cliff and end up mad at God because he didn't hear our prayer. "Faith without works is dead" (James 2:26, King James Version). In the pages to come, I would encourage you to not only level up in your understanding of who God really is in and through you but also to apply the tools and information I so freely give away.

This book contains all the tools I have developed to help *anyone*, "believer" or not, who has fallen asleep to his or her life without recognizing it and needs to wake up to live like the dreamer they are. It's time to bring your piece of heaven to this earth. These are the tools and insights needed to complement everything you already know at a head level and will now give you the opportunity to tap in at a heart level so you can really *do* something about it. As you'll come to learn, the power is not found just in knowing information or quoting God's scripture but in picking up the oars of life, utilizing the sail, and turning on the motor so that you can see His manifested power at work in your life. It only works if you work it.

Keep in mind that dreaming is a process. It is a journey that will require you to *actively* participate in every moment of your life, so I will ask you to be intentional about the information you are reading. Don't just learn it at a head level; learn it at a heart level so you can do something with it. Often. Daily. All the time. We learn best by doing, so don't just read and gain knowledge: **earn the gift of transformation**. All I ask, while you read this book, is to stick with the process. Even on days when you don't see your dreams happening (it's okay, you won't see it at first), when you don't *feel* like you're getting anywhere (your feelings are just information but they aren't hard and fast truth), and when the world around you says, "It's impossible" (they don't know what you know), stick with it. I promise, the art of stick-to-it-ness will absolutely serve you in building a stronger faith as well as a better life, family, career, community, and world, but you can't tap out.

This book is *not* designed to be a feel-good book. Yes, you will feel good at times, but the truth does have this weird way of pissing you off before it makes you feel good. We are going straight for the truth, which will make you re-think everything. It will require you to look at things that maybe you haven't looked at in a long time, or ever, and that's a tough thing to do. It's about starting anew and living a life from a new vantage point.

This book is designed to be a catalyst for change. It will cause you to look at and approach your life differently. It will cause you to make the necessary changes to come into your greatest alignment, and even though exciting, can also be challenging. It's created to support you in wading through the waters of the unknown, which again, isn't easy but necessary if you want different results in your life. This kind of change will also evoke and build reverent fear and responsibility within you because you are about to identify the things that matter most to you. Once you learn what matters most, you can't unlearn it. You will then have to do something with it.

And lastly, this book will give you the opportunity to practice a new way of living. As Malachi, my oldest son, says, "Practice makes better." You have likely practiced life one way for the last ten, twenty, even forty years, so to expect instant results isn't going to be fair. This is going to take some time and intentional practice. Ask me how I know?! Truth be told, I was a *learned* realist and controller. Early on, I taught myself to live this way to protect and shield myself from pain and disappointment. For twenty-five years, day in and day out, I unconsciously convinced myself that "only the strong survive," and the way you stay strong was to disconnect from any emotion or feeling (including my heart) and control anything you possibly could. Since having my own "great awakening," I had to consciously, day in and day out, learn how to get back into my own body and heart with a freak ton of practice. I had to deal with my anger problems, trust issues, and an overactive brain so I could live from a place of purpose and passion. I had to learn how to feel safe in my skin again. I had to learn how to "go in" to hear God's voice and to trust His leading. I had to learn each of the things I'm about to teach you. For these reasons dreaming didn't come easy to me at first, but it ultimately saved my life.

With all that being said, please NOTE: I am not a therapist. If you feel emotionally unstable or unable to do this on your own, PLEASE DON'T. If you feel like you can manage to look at your past and to deal with the pain, then continue; otherwise, please don't. Be mindful.

To each and one of you reading this book, the world needs your dreams because the world needs more people connected to their hearts and therefore connected to God. The world needs God's demonstrated power in a way they've yet to see, and I believe, just like it says in Acts, that as God gives us prophecies, dreams, and visions, it's these dreamers who are going to bring about the change that we all so desperately need. You dreamers are the activists, believers, and change agents in this life. You are the do-gooders and visionaries who will manifest the real demonstration of God's power. You are the entrepreneurs who are ready to execute, the faith-walking go-getters, and not afraid to try-ers who just needed permission to be who you were created to be: permission granted!

From the bottom of my heart, I am indebted to my own crazy dream back in my RV bedroom that literally blew my mind; it gave me the infrastructure to create this message. Thank you to that lady in the women's restroom, wherever you may be, whose response sparked such a fire in my soul that I have since spent hundreds and hundreds of hours writing this book. And thank you to the countless friends and clients who have shared their deepest secrets, fears, desires, and dreams with me. This one is for you! All of you have forced me to press in and figure out the things that I might have just ignored. It has given me a deep reason to uncover, quantify, and research dreaming in all its elements, to sit with myself, to sit with God, to lean in, and to "go in." Here, in the pages to follow, I share *all* my findings, downloads, insights, and tactical tools so you, too, can live the life of your dreams.

Let's do this.

Don't let life get in the way of you living your **DREAMS**. Instead, have a **DREAM** that's louder than your life to live for!

SECTION 1

CREATING AWARENESS

CHAPTER 1

Define Dreaming

DREAMING IS A LOT LIKE DATING. Let's be real, dating is awkward at first. Two people from totally different walks of life are coming together, attempting to share stories without stumbling over their words so as not to look ridiculous. They are wearing their Sunday best, wondering when the right time for the first kiss is, and fretting over whether or not it's too soon to ask for that second date. Then, once they're past that hurdle, they're nervous about introducing family members, and wonder and fret over when it's actually okay to fart in front of each other. They anxiously await the moment that they have to break the news that they actually don't like their date's cooking. You know, all the things. But step by step, the awkward turns into sincerity and the sincerity into something magical and unique.

Dating seems to require that you kiss a few frogs to find the right one. It can often feel like a waste of time, and maybe the thought's even crossed your mind that "this isn't for me" because it does have its bumps in the roads, its ups and downs, challenges, dark times, and disappointments. But the manifestation of true love is one of life's greatest miracles. And just like the path of true love, in all its awkwardness, joy, pain, and yes, even disappointments, dreaming too is one of life's greatest miracles.

Now, depending on when in your life you're reading this book, the years you've experienced leading up to this moment, "the number of frogs" you've kissed, and the number of dreams you've chased, it's likely we have one thing in common. We are all at very different spots as it pertains to dreaming. Regardless of your starting point, it's likely that your position on dreaming is one of the following:

You have never dreamt before. Like, ever.

You have had epic failures pursuing your dreams, so why bother?

You don't have a problem dreaming; you've just never accomplished your dreams, so you feel more like a "hopeless romantic."

You've been living a dream, but you are at the crux of a major transition, and you're starting to feel hopeless because you have no insight into what's next.

You are literally living a current dream and are already excited for the next one so reading this book makes you feel like "party on, Garth."

Or, you have no idea what I'm talking about, but you're intrigued.

Regardless of where you stand today on the topic of dreaming, regardless of your history, your stories, experiences, expectations, upbringing, social status, political views, or favorite flavor of ice cream, you are curious and recognize that you probably need a few more dreams to come true in your life if you're going to get the most out of this life. But where do you start? How do you even make the time to create the life you've always dreamed of?

Maybe it feels like life has just kind of happened to you or is happening to you, so dreaming feels irrelevant and even irresponsible. Perhaps you didn't grow up in an environment that honored the dreaming process, or you're just flat out skeptical about the whole idea. But something has to give because the results you're currently getting are not the ones you want. Maybe you're looking around at the current events happening in your life or on a global scale, and you see the need for change, but where do you begin?

Now, the hardest part about the work we're going to do in this book is the fact that we're all unique, which means our experiences and perspectives are unique. Our approach to life, in general, is unique, yet regardless of how unique we all may be, here's one thing I know to be true: so much of what we experience and feel is universal—love, joy, anger, resentment, fear, doubt, loss, and pain. Although we've all experienced unique aspects of such things, they *are* universal and, in theory, not unique at all. Once we recognize this to be true, we can start to wade through the waters of our differences, finding more in common than not.

With that being said, I will *never* underestimate or overestimate the levels of anger, joy, love, pain, shame, or guilt you are dealing with. That's not my agenda, nor is it my point. However, in each chapter, in every way, I am going to do my best to clarify and "set the stage" as well as I can so we can all begin and venture through this journey together, on the same page. Fair enough?

Let's start with actually defining what dreaming is.

What does it mean to dream?

Many, I'm sure, already have a preconceived notion, opinion, or bias about the idea of dreaming. We all think we know a lot about this subject, but truth be told, we know very little, which is why we're not getting the results we desire.

Upon asking a multitude of people what dreaming means to them, I received a variety of responses such as:

It means nothing to me. It's a pie-in-the-sky approach to life.

I dream when I sleep.

Get real. Life requires us to work, pay bills, and grow old. I don't have time for it.

I used to dream … when I was a kid.

Ha. I'm too busy to dream.

I'm living the dream. I think …

I don't understand the question.

The variety of thought processes, emotions, and opinions around this topic are quite varied, sad, and even hilarious. Because we can view this topic so differently, it can create a chasm in understanding the truth and hinder how we approach it. After researching and considering all the angles involved, the part of the definition I want to focus on is when the word is used as a verb, indicating that beyond being a noun, the word has action. It's important to understand that when a word is used as a verb, it means that it is something that expresses action and a state of being. That means that as you begin to dream, not only will it be expressed in your actions, it will also be expressed in your state of being, you will actually embody it. Dreaming, when used as a verb, can be recognized as the ability to *contemplate* possibilities.

Now, I admit, I am a pretty big activist for words and their meaning because words *and* their definitions matter. It's easy to water down the power of words, but they have more meaning and power than we give them credit. Words hold unbiased truth, making them important to us, we who are not so unbiased and have probably one too many opinions for our own good. Words allow us to look at and ensure we thoroughly understand the true meaning of things, as they actually are, so we can apply them to our lives in ways that *truly* transform our thought processes and habits. Here's what I found as I dug deeper, as I looked at the words within the words:

To have the ability to *contemplate the possibilities* means actually thinking about things in a much deeper, more *thoughtful* way. I would even say it's the ability to consider things in a much more profound way, almost like a *meditative* state. When you're in a state of thoughtfulness you're showing much more care, attention, and consideration to the things around you as well as the things within you. When you're in a *meditative* state, you'll find that you're actually able to focus your mind and attention on a specific focal point for an extended period of time without the distractions of this world getting in the way. This is what allows you to go beyond your day-to-day mental chatter and begin to tap into a much more profound space, actually focusing in on something deeper. It's good to note here that another word for focal point is heart. So if I were to say that again, my statement would read:

Meditation is when you're able to focus your mind and attention *on the heart* for an extended period of time without the distractions of this world getting in the way.

When we come from this thoughtful place, it's easy to be engulfed and totally swept up by it. When we tap into these levels of profound perspective, it's so much richer and more meaningful than we could ever think up on our own. It's so much deeper, like the vastness of the ocean. This is the unchartered territory within you. This is where your dreams are born.

By piecing together all of the above, we are going to work off of my definition, the **JG** definition, of the word dreaming from here on out. Are you ready for this?! Dreaming means:

. . . .

*Great and intense focus, with deep absorption
of thought, in a different realm that brings
about possibilities while considering the
needs of those around you.*

. . . .

In other words, dreaming is the ability to go so dang deep within your-self that you are so in tune with what the Spirit of God is doing, paying so much conscious attention to what's important to you and what He's doing within you, that you'll never go without in the world around you because He's already provided everything you need to accomplish what He's given to you! The Bible says, "And God is able to bless you abundantly, so that in all things at all times, having all that you need, you will abound in every good work" (2 Corinthians 9:8). **Therefore, dreaming God's dream for your life means you've been given a ticket to have anything you need, at any time, and in any way you can fathom or imagine.**

Come on now. If you're not shouting *amen* at me right now, I don't know what else you want from me!

This definition proves how profoundly powerful dreaming is and veri-fies that *it is the key* that will wake you up to your own life. It is the impetus for change.

Maybe you're thinking: "Wait. How? Who? What? I missed it." That's okay. Stick with me on this as we break it down even more so you can see the actual magnitude and power of its meaning. Let's unpack my definition of the word dreaming, bit by bit:

Great and intense focus … When you have great and intense focus, you are awake. You are tuned in. It's like when you get lost, or you're doing a freaking hard workout, giving birth, or challenging yourself beyond normal limits, what happens? You are alert. You are 1,000 percent paying attention! Why? Because what you're doing draws you in and requires all of you, so it gets more, if not all, of your attention. That's the same premise and foundation for dreaming. Being that it is outside your normal thought process, it requires complete and total focus, which means you will never feel bored or unmotivated.

... with deep absorption of thought ... Deep absorption of thought is a meditative state. It is a state beyond the chatter of the mind. Research has shown that deep absorption of thought (i.e., meditation) helps our brain stop processing information because the frontal lobe, the most sophisticated part of our brain responsible for planning, reasoning, emotions, and even our self-conscious awarenesses, goes "offline." That means while in deep absorption of thought, the insecure thoughts that run around in your head, the worry, doubt, and fear you're accustomed to, all just shut off, and you begin to tap into a much deeper level of consciousness. This is also known as "flow." It may not even contain conscious words but rather a gut-knowing that mystifies all reason and understanding. This level of attention is like a muscle, though, and one that needs to be strengthened over time to work at its highest potential.

... in a different realm ... In a different realm means that dreaming happens in a different reality, not the one you are in today, which is a good thing because most of what we see today is not ideal, nor is it what we really want. When you begin to tap into a different realm, you begin the journey of being less dependent on the things you see around you and more concerned with the things you see within you. Most people have it all backward and have given so much oomph to a society that is all about "the see." What I mean by that is we are so tied into what everyone else is doing, has, and thinks about any given topic that we are losing ourselves in the midst of all "the see." Social media has forced this even more. Twenty-four seven, we have the ability to not only check in with what our neighbor is doing but with anyone and everyone associated with our social media accounts. We have conditioned ourselves to be more connected with what everyone else is doing around us that we've lost our connection to what's truly going on within us. Truth be told, what's going on around us is *not* where the power is. The power is in the unseen, in what we cannot see with our natural eye. Dreaming first begins in a different realm because it allows us to manifest what's going on within us regardless of what's happening around us.

... that brings about possibilities ... It means that this is a very active concept. True dreaming literally "brings about." It is not a passive concept. It's not just something we think about or talk about, though people do get stuck in this part of the process (we will talk about why and how in later chapters). It's not about things happening by chance, luck, or because of the lottery. Active participation must take place for dreams to manifest. From the moment the dream comes to you to the moment it is fulfilled, it's a day in and day out, literal, mental, and emotional commitment that requires us to *do* something to *bring about*. This means that true purpose, identity, desire, possibility, and creation are found on the other side of action.

... while considering the needs of those around you. Dreaming is the least selfish thing you could ever do. Many of you need to consider this because you've convinced yourself that dreaming is selfish. You've got yourself on this hamster wheel of an energy suck because you think that your dreams are only for you. As though they will take away from the people you care most about when the reality is, dreaming and the fulfillment of your deepest dreams benefits everybody, *including those you love most.* A true dream takes into consideration the needs of the people around you. Dreams are not full of ego or pride. Rather, dreams are an enlightened perspective signifying a desire to make the world a better place. A dream is not just for you; it's for everyone around you. It doesn't mean a better life just for you; it's a better life for everyone who comes into contact with the fulfillment of that dream. It means that true contribution, community, and connection are on the other side of your dreams. Basically, this tells us that **dreaming is not a selfish activity, but rather becomes selfish when you don't do it!**

This is what dreaming is all about at its very essence and core.

As we move forward, every time I mention the word dreaming, we can share in the purest, truest definition of the word to let it transform our lives. Hang onto this. Build from this place as we progress.

As we begin, what I want you to do first is consider where you're at in your dreaming process. It's hard to envision where you are going or what might be possible when you don't even know where you are. So first things first, I want to give you space and permission to hear yourself and to identify "Where am I?"

I encourage you to answer the following questions:

Where am I at in my dreaming process?

_____

_____

_____

What do I consider my current truth about dreaming to be?

_____

_____

_____

Does the truth I have about dreaming serve me? If so, can I commit to keeping it? If it doesn't serve me, can I commit to finding a truth about dreaming that will serve me? If so, what could that new truth be?

_____

_____

_____

Where am I at with the relationship I have with myself? How do I see myself? How do I treat myself?

_____

_____

_____

Where am I at with the relationship I have with God? Who do I say God is? What role does He play in my life and in the life of my dreams?

_____

_____

_____

What dreams do I have within me right now? Despite failure or success, acceptance or rejection, right or wrong, what do I *wish* for my life? What's most important to me? What do I want more than anything? (Don't overthink this one too much. Do NOT take into consideration any external influences—brother, cousin, mom, spouse—let this be about you and you alone.)

_____

_____

_____

Why do I want to live the life of my dreams?

_____

_____

_____

And last but not least: Am I willing? Am I willing to learn? Willing to *know*? Willing to wake up?

_____

_____

_____

A true
DREAM takes
into consideration the
needs of the people
around you, which
means, it's the least
selfish thing you
could ever do.

CHAPTER 2

The Power of Dreaming (and Why We MUST Do It)

WE ALL HAVE DREAMS. Every single one of us. It's one of the few things we as humans have in common. We dream of living and loving more passionately. We dream of choice, freedom, and a truer way to live. We dream of creating change and lasting impact. We dream of more personal fulfillment and peace. We dream of a career we can be proud of, relationships that are more connected, a community that's more engaged, and a world that does good.

So if we *all* have dreams, why do so few of us actually *live the dream*? Like that elderly woman in the bathroom, why has "living the dream" become more of a sarcastic phrase than actual reality?

If I were to ask you, "What stops *you* from actually *living the dream?*" What would your answer be? Write your response here:

_____

_____

_____

When most are asked this question, the universal response is, "Life. Life stops me from living the dream." If we stop and digest the magnitude of this answer, it's soul-crushing, because if "life" stops us from living the dream, then what's the point of life?! Jesus even says, "I have come that they may have life, and have it to the full" (John 10:10).

But life happens. Our perceptions, biases, and judgments jade our perspective. Our environments, what we "see," and what we "know" keep us from the real truth because we're unconsciously committed to the habits we've created, whether they serve us or not. Our friends, acquaintances, family, and even social media, YouTube, and the news have all of a sudden shaped our perspectives of what's possible versus impossible. Our anxiety, worry, doubt, and fear is so distracting that it's *killing* our ability to believe, let alone dream, and so many of us are physically and emotionally in survival mode, which is using so much of our energy that we don't have more to spend on progression and advancement, let alone dreaming. Yet, we know, deep down, there has to be more. *There's got to be more, right?!*

Right.

The Bible says, "Though seeing, they do not see; though hearing, they do not hear or understand. In them is fulfilled the prophecy of Isaiah: 'You will be ever hearing but never understanding; you will be ever seeing but never perceiving'" (Matthew 13:13-14). Why? Because as it goes onto say, "For this people's heart has become calloused; they hardly hear with their ears, and they have closed their eyes. Otherwise they might see with their eyes, hear with their ears, understand with their hearts and turn, and I would heal them" (Matthew 13:15). So in most cases, it's not that God isn't speaking; it's that we aren't positioning ourselves to hear Him.

My question to you is this: Are you ready to hear?

If the answer is yes, let's continue by looking at the power behind dreaming.

Why is there POWER in dreaming?!

There are two reasons why there is so much power in dreaming:

1. **Our dreams are connected to our hearts, not our heads.**

2. **We are *created* to *create*.**

Our dreams are connected to our hearts, not our heads, which is why I say that dreaming is not for the faint of heart but rather for those of heart. The Bible says, "Trust in the Lord with all your *heart* and lean not on your own *understanding*" (Proverbs 3:5 [emphasis mine]). There is a reason why.

When I refer to the heart, and this space within you (heart space), what I'm referring to is your spirit and soul. It is the deep *knowing*. It's the still, small voice inside you. It's your gut, your intuition, that nudge that you feel. It's the very voice of God *in you*. "For those who are led by the Spirit of God are the children of God" (Romans 8:14).

When we are led from this place, when we follow His voice, that nudge, we are partnering with and bringing our slice of heaven to this earth. That's why when the Bible says, "Set your hearts on things above" (Colossians 3:1), it means it is because your dreams come straight from this place. It's when we align ourselves with what heaven is doing, and with what God is dreaming, that our own dreams are born.

From this space, imagination and creation are birthed. This space within you is able to live open, untethered, uninhibited, unconditional, never self-seeking, and full of life, love, and unending possibilities because it is connected to itself and to God. It is forgiving, forbearing, and without limitations. This is why the Bible says, "Above all else, guard your heart, for *everything* you do flows from it" (Proverbs 4:23 [emphasis mine]). Your heart is the very seed of your life.

The more aware of this space you are, the more you recognize that it doesn't function at an intellectual level because this heart space exists outside the confines and understanding of the intellect, often making it hard to understand at a head level. This is why words and insights don't always make logical sense. This space doesn't speak in the words of man but rather in images, colors, or in deep-seated revelations and ideas that just kind of plop in your lap. What you see at this level isn't yet seen with the physical eye, so it's necessary to learn how to be aware of it and how to trust it. "As it is written, 'What no eye has seen, what no ear has heard, and what no human mind has conceived'—the things God has prepared for those who love him" (1 Corinthians 2:9).

It's where your real power comes from and where all the magic happens. It's the place where building a better world is built *not* because of what you see around you or what you've experienced, but because of what you *know*, sense, and can feel within you. It's how you're able to go where you've never been and do what you've never done because your dreams are outside the mind's mental conditioning and analytics. Your dreams take you where the mind cannot and will not go. The Bible says, "This new plan I'm making with Israel isn't going to be written on paper, isn't going to be chiseled in stone; This time "I'm writing out the plan *in them*, carving it *on the lining of their hearts*" (Hebrews 10:16, MSG [emphasis mine]).

In this place, your heart, like heaven, doesn't have timelines. It has no expectations or attachments; it simply *knows*, therefore, holding within it infinite truth. Your heart lives *without* judgment and critical nature. It doesn't even know how to compare or feel mocked. The Bible says, "I consider that our present sufferings are not worth comparing with **the glory that will**

be revealed within us. For the creation waits in eager expectation for the children of God to be revealed" (Romans 8:18–19 [emphasis mine]). There is glory on the inside of you! This is where your dreams live. No one else holds the insight to unleashing these dreams, and no one else holds the keys to unlocking them within you, besides you. It's like a treasure chest waiting to be opened.

That suggests the question, if this space is so powerful, magical, and insightful, like a treasure chest waiting to be opened, why would one choose *not* to open it? Why are we not living from this space, from the heart?

It's often less about not opening the treasure chest of dreams but more about a blockage that occurs.

How do we become blocked?

We become blocked because of hurt. Our hurt compounds and becomes unprocessed pain, and unprocessed pain wreaks havoc on our lives because we become disconnected and out of alignment.

Consider I'm out playing on the skateboard with my kids, and being that I'm not real coordinated (I'm good at other things), I fall and bang up my elbow pretty badly. Perhaps I acknowledge it for a second, but then I keep going on with my life, ignoring the pain, covering up the wound but doing nothing to heal it. What do you think is bound to happen? Infection. What started as a wound (hurt) becomes a huge issue in my life (unprocessed pain). The same is true for us in areas of emotional hurt.

The minute we are hurt or become emotionally wounded, what do we do? We close ourselves off. We literally shut ourselves off to the world. We shut down the intimacies within ourselves too. God? Yep, we close ourselves off to Him also. Why? Because now, even intimacy seems scary. The Bible says, "The Lord is close to the brokenhearted," (Psalm 34:18) but if you're anything like me, after being hurt, that sounds scarier than it sounds relieving. And instead of living with heart, we begin to live with hurt—bottled up hurt.

This is how we become blocked. It's our hurt, turned into unprocessed pain that we begin to use as a shield to protect ourselves. Just as Adam and Eve hid in the Garden of Eden, literally shielding themselves from God, thinking they were protecting themselves, we do the same thing. We think we're guarding our heart, but really, we're just blocking our treasure from being released. This ultimately becomes a huge reason why we aren't living our dreams—because we're blocking our heart and a blocked heart means unfulfilled dreams.

This blockage also causes us to no longer live from heart but rather from head—within the very confines of our own mind chatter and brain, where we are no longer able to see "the picture in the frame." This leads to a very controlled, fearful, and analytical approach to how we live our lives because your head can only conjure up things it can conceive, understand, or has already experienced. In contrast your heart space taps into the yet to be seen, heard, imagined, or invented (i.e., the impossible) space. This is why it's easy to lose trust in God because "logically, He doesn't make any sense." Your head then begins to take over and starts defining things as wrong versus right and puts things (including people) into categories. Your heart doesn't do that. Your head fears judgment and the great unknown. It reasons with itself and can paint some crazy mental images when facing obstacles. Your heart doesn't do that. However, after being hurt or emotionally wounded, we unconsciously no longer trust our hearts to lead us; we trust our head. We trust our logic and, ultimately, our fears, worries, and doubts, therefore giving up our freedom for safety, security, and stability. We call it "comfort," but as quoted in *The Greatest Showman*, "Comfort is the enemy of progress."

Most of the time, people who say they "can't dream" don't realize that it's not that they *can't* but rather that they have literally wired and conditioned their mind and brain not to. *It's a learned state*, but it doesn't have to be permanent. You have learned to live in your head. This tells me you can also unlearn it by simply learning something new, and in order to dream, you're going to have to. To access the dreams within you, you're going to have to learn the difference between your heart and your head, and you're going to have to learn how to master your mind, something we will do extensively in Chapter 6. The bottom line is, in order to dream, your head cannot be the central point in your life.

You will also have to learn how to heal at a heart level because it's from the cry of your heart that your dreams will be born, set free, and manifested. Now, when I talk about living from heart, I'm not talking about just any kind of heart. I'm talking about a *whole* heart. Note: I will reference the word "whole" throughout this entire book.

What does it mean to have a *whole* heart?

When we consider what whole actually means, we'd conclude that it means *all* of something because we find words like entirety and complete. Whole means that something is in one piece. Therefore, a *whole* heart is a heart in one piece. It's complete, undivided, unbroken, and undamaged, which means it is aligned! This is why you have to heal. Because if you're not healed, you're not whole, and if you're not whole, you're likely to feel incomplete, broken, and detached; and frankly, that is no way to live life, let alone manifest your dreams.

They say that "Time heals everything," but I couldn't disagree more. Time doesn't heal everything. Healing heals everything. By healing your hurt and processing your pain, which we will do in this book, you can begin to live from heart. You unblock yourself. New thoughts, creative ideas, growth, change, wisdom, clarity, real insight, and yes, even "God ideas" (as I call them) begin to emerge from this space. From this space, you begin to think new thoughts, which fires neurons in the brain that begin to work together, making new pathways of intellectual understanding. All of this enables you as a dreamer to be that much more fluid in your approach, unapologetic if you will, bold, courageous, and sure, still nervous (you are human), but much more assertive in who you are and about the things you want to create. This brings me to my next point. The second reason dreaming is so powerful is because we are actually created to create.

We are *created* to *create*. Many don't see themselves as a creator, yet alone creative. We have an unconscious identity, and "creator" is not it. We call ourselves "logical," "analytical," "a realist." Fair, unless it's prohibiting you from being the creator you were born to be.

On top of that, many of us have learned and even trained ourselves to live on autopilot somewhere along the line. We are reacting to life, responding to things as they come, unaware of what's going on within us, stuck in habits and routines, and likely to do as we're told or at least do things the way we've always done them without giving any real thought as to *why*. We go to school, graduate, go to college, get a degree, fall into our job and stay for no other reason than to make money, get married, buy the house, have the kids, and continue to live much of our lives with unchecked and even unprocessed pain, thought processes and emotions. Then we wonder why we wake up in our thirties, forties, and fifties, asking, "Is there something more?"

We started following the rules and doing as we were told without giving any thought to the fact that maybe, just maybe, there was a different way and without understanding why we're doing what we're doing, which means we're definitely not tapping into an enlightened state. However, you will find that you were *born to create*, not just follow the rules, especially as you lean into this work.

Our Creator is a creator, and in His image, we, too, were created. Which means you were not born just to respond and react to this life, to work at a job simply to pay bills, or to go along with societal norms just because that's how things are done or what's expected of you, but to really enter this life as a creator and contributor. This is why we are too often functioning but mildly depressed, bored, anxious, depleted, or lacking motivation because we aren't creating. Anytime anything isn't being utilized for its core purpose, it lacks fulfillment and satisfaction. I, personally, in my own seasons of unclear purpose, even felt *literal* pain, like a part of me was missing. Some have even mentioned to me this feeling of "being parched," and others admitted to feeling out of control, sad, apathetic, and lacking in motivation. Perhaps you can relate. Maybe it feels like deep sadness or ongoing irritability, constant fatigue, or difficulty concentrating and focusing; maybe you feel unhappy, angry, or even anxious; maybe you lack energy, are craving unhealthy food or old addictions, or are isolating yourself because you feel helpless and depressed. You're not alone. Fifteen million people per year, at any given time, in America alone, admit to having minor to major issues with depression. Now, I'm no doctor, and I'm not suggesting you not take your recommended meds, but for me, even when I was in my darkest, depressive state, had I walked into a doctor's office, they might have prescribed me with a hefty dose of who knows what. But the reality was that a pill was not going to change me from the inside out. It might have numbed the pain and confusion for a minute, but it wasn't going to heal the pain I felt inside. I didn't need a pill. I needed a dream bigger than my life to live for.

We weren't created just to respond, be reactive, or coast through life. We were created for so much more, and yet, at times, if we're not careful, we look at ourselves and our lives as though life is just happening to us and we are along for the ride, without ample consideration of the fact that we've been given all the tools to make life what we want it to be.

All of us, in every way, were designed to create. "God created mankind in his own image, in the image of God he created them" (Genesis 1:27). This principle is magical, *and* it's our responsibility. If we are made in the image of God and God is a creator, why would we ever think we weren't given everything we need to also be a creator? "Before I formed you in the womb I knew you, before you were born I set you apart" (Jeremiah 1:5). God is brilliant in that He gave each of us individualized purpose, and it's in our dreaming that our purpose is released. Many say, "I don't know what my purpose is," and I always say to that, "Dream and you'll find out quickly what it is." The manifestation of your dreams is a part of your purpose. It's what you're here to do. It's your piece of heaven that you are bringing to this earth. That means your purpose *is* within reach when you spend your life pursuing and manifesting your dreams.

Now, that doesn't mean it's going to be easy, nor does it mean that all of life will just fall into place, but it does mean you have the capacity and the capabilities to turn things around, and that is an amazing feeling. Yes, there are aspects to life you *cannot* control: the weather, other people, death, market crashes, sickness, etc. but these things do not have to define you. When you see yourself as a creator instead of falling prey to the things around you and letting life's circumstances write your future, you can *overcome by creating*. If you don't see "it," create "it."

Just because you don't see it or don't have it doesn't mean it's impossible. It just means you haven't created it *yet*. Just because a better life wasn't modeled for you growing up doesn't mean you can't dream it and then create it. Just because you didn't have a mom or a dad who treated you the way you wanted to be treated does not mean you have to be the same kind of parent. Dream up who you want to be to your kids and then create it. Dream up the kind of career you want and either go get it or build it yourself. You may feel like you are a product of your environment, but it doesn't mean you have to stay that way. You are way too good for that! Create the career you want, create the marriage or relationship you want, create the home, the adventure, and the kind of health you want. Dream it. Then, create it.

It's not letting life just happen to you, nor is it about just responding to whatever comes at you. It's not about leaving things up to chance or falling prey to a victim mentality that says, "It happens *to* me." No, life is here for us to engage, to interact with it, to taste, see, feel, and touch that it is good. If we don't like something, we have the innate potential and ability to find a different, better, and more beneficial way to do something. All of this becomes possible when you see yourself as a creator.

Let's look at a few examples of true dreamers that exemplify both points, that dreaming comes from heart (not head), and that we are born to create— examples I will use throughout this book:

Martin Luther King Jr. Talk about a man with a dream. The power behind Martin Luther King Jr.'s dream is that he did *not* see it anywhere *around* him when he first started, but he did see it *within* him. Liberty and freedom for all races did not exist when he started. Think about what it was like to be him, considering the times he was in, speaking out as a black man in a way that publicly declared something unheard of, protested, and even shunned. Can you imagine getting up in front of hundreds and hundreds of people, time and time again, going public with your dream that literally nobody understood?!

Most of us can't even do that in the quiet of our own home, let alone in the public eye, while being shunned for the color of your skin, while doing it in love and with good motive, living it out unapologetically, and ultimately dying for it. I mean for real. Imagine that, dying for your dream. But he had a dream, and because of the conviction of his dream, he became an unstoppable force that changed history.

His life confirmed that he didn't see himself as a taker; he was a creator. He didn't believe in sitting back and letting life "play out" but rather felt led to be a force for good, to *create* liberty in a way that hadn't yet been created. Just because he didn't see it didn't mean it was impossible.

Desmond T. Doss is another example. Here was a man who is known for saving seventy-five men during the bloodiest battle of WWII and the only conscientious objector to receive the Medal of Honor. I first learned about him in the movie *Hacksaw Ridge* where he is portrayed as a man living his dreams from sheer conviction (something we will talk a lot about in Chapter 9). Here was a man who enlists into the army as a combat medic, refusing to bear arms because he believed that while everyone else was taking lives, he was going to save them.

As you watch the movie, it's the most heroic decision that is tested time and time again, and yet, despite the heartache, isolation, judgment, and brutal force used against him by his own team, he still chooses what's right. He sees something that nobody else can see. It's not until he saves seventy-five men, literally dragging their bodies off the battlefield in the middle of the war, in the dead of the night when all others had retreated, with Japanese soldiers unleashing havoc on him, without bearing arms, that people finally begin to understand his dream.

Sure, to others, what he committed to didn't make any logical sense, and yet, he was willing to give up his life and his freedom to stay true to what he believed. Because he held a dream so deep within himself and felt responsible for enlisting as a combat medic who does not take up arms, he found the power, stamina, and ability to persevere. This is another beautiful example of someone who chose to live from heart, not head, to be a creator in this life and not just a follower.

Jason Russell is another amazing example. He is one of the greatest activists of our time who, as a college kid, traveled to Uganda to "find a story" and ended up finding a calling. Upon traveling and aimlessly wandering for three weeks, he and his buddies finally stumbled upon the story of a lifetime—children, traveling at night, every night, to escape the hands of the Lord's Resistance Army (LRA). Hundreds of children's stories and severe pain had gone untold until Russell and his team made it their life's story to share the children's unspeakable truth. For ten years, Invisible Children fought to tell the story of Joseph Kony and the inexplicable devastation he was creating through the LRA.

At the starting line, Russell and the team at Invisible Children had no business being in this industry. They had no experience ending a war and had no credibility in getting people to listen, but it was their deep-seated dream that turned this hell on earth into a story never to forget. After ten years, thousands of supporters, millions of views on their YouTube channel, and sheer commitment to creating awareness programs, Russell and his team sat in the Oval Office with President Obama and signed the "Lord's Resistance Army Disarmament and Northern Uganda Recovery Act," which was a piece of legislation that deployed 100 U.S. soldiers to advise local forces to track and capture Kony.

I guarantee you there were countless times that Russell and his team thought: THIS IS CRAZY, and at a head level and even a peer level, they would be right. They had a ton to risk, including their safety and sanity, and despite the praise and criticism they've received over the years, they went even deeper within themselves and found something bigger to live for. Their dream was bigger than their own safety and security, and because of that level of commitment, they are *creating* a way where there was no way. And even though the war still sadly continues, and Kony is not arrested, the amount of continued progress and commitment by Invisible Children is unbreakable.

Believe it or not, **you are no different.** You have the same potential on the inside of you to manifest the same thing. The *only* one who needs to be convinced is you.

You'll quickly learn that it's not about *you* having a dream but rather a dream *having* you, your *whole* heart. It took Martin Luther King Jr. bringing his *whole* heart to share his story. It took Jason Russell and the entire team at Invisible Children, each bringing their *whole* heart to share their story. Doss? Yep, same deal, *whole* heart.

Will you tell the full story of who you are and what's important to you with your *whole* heart? Will you quiet the chatter of your mind and step into the role as a creator of your own life so you can make it what you dream versus more of what it already is?

Even if your heart feels as though it's been shattered in two, disappointed, or misled, it's okay. With every dream you create, it's almost like righting every wrong. By dreaming, you make amends with your past, you learn to trust your future, and you settle into the present moment. You take what you can't see, and you create something you can. What's impossible becomes possible, and the pain, in time, is beautifully turned into purpose. It's the most incredible journey you'll take in your lifetime. *And* sure, it's hard as hell, but what's the alternative, to sit in your pain and just keep reliving it? No thank you.

And sure, it's going to cost you. You didn't think it would be easy, did you?! I don't mean to sound crass, but I do want you to consider the cost because dreaming will cost you. Purpose will cost you. Vision will cost you. But so does a life of mediocrity, justification, avoidance, anger, and resentment. It's all going to cost you something and fortunately and unfortunately, you *do* have to pick. You are going to have to pick a side. Dreaming does not suddenly make life perfect or even easier; it just makes it worth living.

Are you ready to take your stance?

Are you ready to take your position?

After reading this book, I don't want you just to *see*; I want you to have a greater *vision*. I don't want you just to *hear*; I want you to *listen*. I don't want you to survive; I want you to thrive. I don't just want you to go through the motions, being reactive to this life; I want you to live life and to go for it, all of it! I don't want you to have a nice dream; I want a dream to have you.

That's the power of your dreams, my friend. You need your dreams. The world needs your dreams. Now, truth be told, to quiet the chatter so we can live from and actually hear our hearts speak, we have to heal our hearts because for many of us, perhaps even all of us, our hearts have been broken a time or two. But that doesn't mean they can't be healed. The rest of this book is designed to prepare you and walk you through your own healing journey so you can create uninhibitedly from the most powerful place within—your heart.

Now, it's up to you to make the choice. But, before we begin, and as a reminder that I would never have you do something I wouldn't do first, let *me* share with you my dreams:

I dream that anyone, and I do mean *everyone,* who comes in contact with me, my work, my business, and my projects is impacted enough to create a life where they did everything that was in their heart to do.

I dream of creating a movement of dreamers who gather together and in unison show the world what it means to live awake, alive, and aligned.

I dream of a logical, analytical, survival-minded world built on statistics, reasons, and excuses to be turned upside down by passion, purpose, a deep fire, and unapologetic dreamers.

I dream of creating a better world for my kids, and yours, by all of us as parents proactively leading from example, simply showing our kids how to be dreamers by the way we choose to live our lives, before our kids are told or believe anything different.

I dream of a world where we no longer compare ourselves to one another or disconnect from ourselves but rather live this human experience with truth and love.

I dream of all of us *knowing,* at a heartfelt level, that we are deeply loved and profoundly important, and therefore, we live like it.

I dream of a world that's turned its pain into purpose, and we're able to recognize that we are all free, that we can create uninhibitedly and without self-limitations.

I dream of a world where we see God as good and life as a gift.

I dream of heaven on earth.

I dream that you take my dare: I DARE YOU TO DREAM.

Your DREAM is
not about
the DREAM.
the DREAM is
about you... It's
about you becoming
all that God intended
for you to be.

CHAPTER 3

The Juxtaposition of Dreaming

AS WE BEGIN THE DREAMING PROCESS, I think it's fundamentally important to wrap your head around what I call the four tools in your toolbox that support you in creating awareness. These are foundational principles that will not only help you *obtain* your dreams but will also guide you in *sustaining* them because, as you'll come to learn, it's one thing to achieve your dreams, and it's another to maintain them.

Per dreaming, I'm after both. I want you to not only get clear and *obtain* your dreams, but I also want you to keep and *sustain* them as well, and in order to do that, these next four chapters will reveal four very important principles (tools) that you will need to take with you on the journey. I will refer back to them often. Here's the first one:

Dreaming is a juxtaposition.

Only we didn't know that.

This very fact is at the root cause of why many people don't dream in the first place. It's why people give up after they get started, and it's truly one of the greatest roadblocks to the manifestation of your dreams. Once you understand how much of a juxtaposition dreaming really is, you'll hopefully not feel so caught off guard when you feel the effects of it. I'll say it again (because that's what all people do when they're trying to drive a point home):

Dreaming is a juxtaposition.

Great JG, what the heck does that mean and how in the world does that help me in the dreaming process?

Here's how this pertains. A juxtaposition happens when you place two things together that have obvious, contradictory effects. That means, what you're dreaming of and what your current reality says to be true *is* going to be two completely different things, very contradictory in effect. No matter the size or the quantity of the dreams you hold within you, they are likely not seen, felt, or experienced in the world around you, or at least not in *your* world. If they were, they wouldn't be your dreams. They would be your reality. Do you see what I mean?

So, for example, let's say you dream of being a successful business owner who sells cool, innovative products while making a difference in the lives of your community. Your dream is to be your own boss, captain of your ship, feeling as though you're finally controlling your destiny (or at least how you spend your day). But, your reality tells you that on paper you aren't experienced enough, you don't have the right degree, you have too messy of a past, you've failed too many times, and you've currently got a crap job with no ability to grow. You've got very little money in your bank account even to buy groceries, let alone start your own business. In comparison to your reality, this dream is in *contradiction* to what you're actually experiencing today.

Or, let's say one of your greatest dreams is to be in a loving, passionate, thriving relationship, but you grew up in a very dysfunctional and disconnected environment. Your current reality says you can't even stay in a short-term relationship, let alone a long-term one. You're broke, living in your parent's basement, and you've convinced yourself that you probably won't amount to much more than your brothers and sisters who are also broke and have no hope or vision or spouses—quite the contradiction.

Perhaps you dream of being healthy, full of energy, 140 pounds, in great shape, and wise with your food choices—the whole nine yards. However, your reality says it's gotten away from you. You're fifty pounds overweight, have no idea what to buy at the grocery store, you've lost weight before but never been able to keep it off, and frankly it feels so overwhelming that you don't even know where to start.

What you want and what you have aren't lining up. It's two contradictory things being seen close together with contrasting effects (ie., juxtaposition).

Here's the truth about dreaming: your dreams and your reality aren't going to line up on day 1 or even day 375. They're not going to line up initially, and frankly, they're not supposed to. The fact of the matter is, your dreams and your reality won't line up until you've actually accomplished the dream itself. It will serve you to stop thinking that your dreams should manifest prematurely and instead, begin to trust the dream and the process even more because *dreaming is a process,* for a very specific reason. It's not just about the destination and what you acquire when you get there. Dreaming is about who you become along the way, something we'll talk further about in the next chapter, *Lifting 'til Failure.*

Knowing all of this supports you because you begin to see the juxtaposition as a gift because now **dreaming is NOT about making a believer out of someone else; dreaming is about making a believer out of you.** The path to accomplishing your dreams is hard, no questions asked. It takes work, vulnerability, patience, perseverance, creativity, and huge levels of trust and faith. It has nothing to do with the people around you; it has to do with you. It requires *you* to tap into the deepest parts of yourself and learn how to trust the desires of your heart and find the conviction required to chase anything important to you even when you don't see it at the starting line—remember, that's normal. No one else can get you on that path, and no one else will be able to keep you on it. This means *you* have to want it badly enough to see past the juxtaposition, past the current reality, past the contrasting effects.

Therefore, this isn't about anyone else. "They" (whoever that is), quite frankly, will *believe* it when they *see* it. But what about you? *Will you believe it BEFORE you see it?* This is key! "Because you have seen me, you have believed; blessed are those who have not seen and yet have believed" (John 20:29).

The Bible tells us, "You are the salt of the earth… You are the light of the world" (Matthew 5:13-14). I think it's easy to preach these verses, but it's not until we consider the juxtaposition that it creates for us that we can apply them to all facets of our life. Consider this: To be the salt of the earth means we are designed to bring about a thirst in others for the Lord. And being that we are the salt of the earth, where do you think we are purposefully placed? In a bland, tasteless environment. Why? Because it's a bland, tasteless environment that needs the salt the most. Quite the contradictory effects, eh?

If we are called to be the light of the world, guess where we are likely to be placed? In a dark world. Why? So the core purpose of the light can be utilized. But what happens if we take that same light and turn it on in an already lit room, can you tell the effect? Hardly. Barely. But if you take that light and put it in a dark room, can you see it's effect? Absolutely. So I'm curious, why are we so impacted by the effect, by the juxtaposition, of us being in a dark world when that's exactly how we do our job?

We pray to be the light, we're placed in a dark world, and what are our unconscious tendencies? To freak out. To pull back. To blame God. We begin to feel inferior, fearful, and worried. This is our wake-up call. Be careful what you pray for. Be careful what you dream of because God knows exactly where to place you to develop and refine that prayer, dream, and core purpose.

If God has put within you an unrest for poverty, an uneasiness about inequality, or a passion for progress and advancement, where do you think He's going to place you? Likely in the middle of it all: poverty, inequality, and stagnation. Right smack-dab in the juxtaposition. Why? Because within you lies the solutions to the problems you're facing. Now, are you going to see the solution on day one? Nope. Day three hundred? Maybe not. But I guarantee you this, if you do nothing and only avoid the awkwardness of the juxtaposition, you're never going to get the solution or the manifestation of your greatest dreams, so you've got to catch the contrasting effects before they catch you.

Let's look at this more specifically in light of your own life. I want you to write down a few of your biggest dreams (I don't care literally how big or small those dreams are; I just want them to be *real* to you). Okay, go ahead, write them down:

Once you're done with that, I want you to take inventory of your current reality. State the obvious. What's going on around you that makes those dreams seem illogical, ridiculous, or unachievable? Take inventory of your reality:

It's likely (and pretty much guaranteed) that the difference between the things you wrote down is polarizing. It's glaringly obvious. It's like oil and water, water and fire. Great. No big deal. It is what it is. Remember, your current reality has no bearing on your dreams, so you're in luck.

I will say it again: *your current reality has no bearing on your dreams.*

Just because your reality doesn't line up or look as if it's in support of your dreams doesn't mean jack squat. AND... AND!! And, instead of wasting so much energy in the middle of the juxtaposition, shaming yourself or blaming God (this is where we lose much of our precious energy), I am going to suggest that you walk *through* the juxtaposition. This can save you a lot of time, energy, and heartache and get you to where you want to be.

Here are two steps to walk you *through* the juxtaposition:

Step 1: Look at both your dream and your reality *exactly* for what they are, nothing more, nothing less. Great. You actually just did that. You looked at your reality for what it is, not what it "should be," not what it "could be," just for what it is. Do not dig holes of shame and guilt. Do not build walls of blame, anger, or frustration. Separate yourself and your own identity from all of it, and just let it be what it is, on paper. If your financial state is bleak, okay, let it be what it is. If you are overweight, okay, let it be what it is. If you've had a really hard past, let it be what it is. If you are going through a divorce, let it be what it is, whatever it is. There's no point in making it worse or giving it more attention and power than you already have. Let it be exactly what it is, nothing more and nothing less. This is being a realist only without all the unnecessary baggage (emotions and judgment) that can come along with it.

Next, look at your dreams for what they are. Don't reason with them, don't try to figure out *how*, don't analyze them, and don't even let your mind chatter about them. At this point in the process, none of that will serve you in manifesting them. Instead, let go of expectations and timelines. Free yourself of when, who, what, where, how, and any other questions that may arise. All I want you to do is to write down every single dream you have within you. Close your eyes if you have to. Sense them. Feel them. *Know* them. And then let them be. This is being a visionary, *the ability to see with imagination and wisdom*. It's having the fortitude to see at a much deeper level. For now, leave both on the pages of this book. Do not compare them. Just let them be. Write those dreams here (and don't worry, if you have a hard time visualizing or identifying your dreams, we'll come back to this part of the process):

Step 2: Pick your hard. When it comes down to two different options or when you're presented with two different choices (i.e., juxtaposition), instead of looking for the easier choice, or thinking that your choice should be easy, or that God should just hand you the answer, why don't you look for and consciously pick the hard that you want most? Here's the truth: it's all hard. Dreaming is hard. Reality is hard. Being single is hard. Being married is hard. Working for someone else is hard. Working for yourself is hard. Having no money is hard. Having a lot of money is hard. Being fat is hard. Being fit is hard. Dreaming is hard. Not living your dream, living someone else's dream, or living half the dream is hard. The bottom line is that it's *all* hard, so rather than searching for the path of least resistance, the goal should be to consciously pick the hard that will get you the results you crave most. Pick the hard that will make you better, smarter, wiser, kinder, more empathetic, and give you the skills you need as you expand your capacity. Pick the hard that satisfies more than just your ego, and go for the one that holds the keys to your true joy and happiness, satisfaction, progression, and fulfills your life's purpose. Pick *that* hard. Look at your reality and look at your dream and consciously pick one. You're already unconsciously choosing, every day, in every way, so you might as well engage consciousness and pick the one you want more. You do this by simply asking the question: *What do I want most?*

Your reality will say one thing; your dream will say another.

Your head will say one thing; your heart will say another.

Your past will say one thing; your future will say another.

Fear will say one thing; faith will say something else.

Doubt will say one thing; courage will say another.

This world will say one thing; God's Word will say another.

Once you recognize the juxtaposition, it becomes a bit simpler to move forward. Notice, I said *simpler*, not *easier*. Just because it's *simple* does not make something *easy*, and again, we are not in it for the easy. We are in it for what we want *most*.

Once you consciously look at your reality and your dreams for what they are, fully committing to choose your dreams *despite* what your current reality says, then it's time to do a few reps to build some muscle, if you will.

DREAMING is
NOT about making
a believer out
of someone else;
DREAMING
is about making a
believer out of you.

CHAPTER 4

Lifting 'Til Failure

DO YOU KNOW THOSE CONVERSATIONS IN LIFE that seem to change everything? Like somehow, it's in one spoken truth bomb that the effects of a misguided truth (i.e., a lie) all of a sudden dissipate, and you're left only with the obvious answer. An answer you had been searching for what feels like a lifetime? And yet, even when you finally have your answer, you feel more flustered and caught off guard than the side effects of just not knowing? Do you know what I'm talking about?

Yeah, I had one of those conversations with my husband midway through our RV travels. And I'll never forget it either.

I had just gotten done at the gym. I was standing near the front door of our RV, Travis was sitting down at the table, and the kids were playing outside in the dirt. It had been over a year since I had given birth to Nixon, our third child, and I was intentionally trying to put on muscle. I have always been a skinnier type, but I have never really been toned or carried much muscle mass, so I was really *trying* to change that. *Trying* being the keyword because I wasn't proactively seeking outside help or insight. I was mainly doing it within my own knowledge base and control, which tells you exactly how most of my results were turning out. Anyhoo, after months of what I considered to be strong, intentional workouts, I finally said to my husband, "I don't know what it is, but I just don't feel like I am gaining as much muscle mass as I should be based upon the frequency and level of intensity in my workouts." Truth be told, I hadn't changed a whole lot about how I was working out. I was just doing *more* of the same thing. Side note, doing *more* of the same thing will never get you *different* results. I continued to go on and on about everything I was doing, all the things I wasn't doing, and was positioning the conversation as more of a "vent session" than a "give me feedback session." I don't think he gave it much profound thought. He might not have even looked up from what he was doing, but after I had gone on for well over ten minutes, out rolled a truth bomb I will never forget. "Are you lifting 'til failure?" he asked.

"Am I what?!" I thought.

Am I lifting 'til failure? What the heck does that mean? And who the heck does he think I am?

But by gosh, given ten seconds of thought, he was completely right. NO, I wasn't lifting 'til failure. I was lifting 'til I was sort of uncomfortable. I was lifting 'til I was kind of sweating. Was I "lifting 'til failure?" NOOOOOOOOO!

How great an example does that paint for all of us? Are we lifting 'til failure, in any area of our lives? If we're honest, probably not. . We are lifting until we are sort of, kind of, uncomfortable. We are lifting 'til we don't want to anymore. We are lifting 'til we want to do something different. We are lifting 'til it's hard, and then we stop. We are lifting to fit our own levels of comfort, but lifting 'til failure? No. The problem with this approach is that we are missing the entire benefit of muscle gain. You might be burning calories and staying thin, no harm, no foul there, but you are not building muscle.

This is the second tool in your toolbox of creating awareness: **lifting 'til failure**.

As mentioned before, **dreams are not just about obtaining. They're not just about "staying skinny"; they're about maintaining and sustaining; they're about gaining strength.**

Your dreams are unlikely to be easy to achieve or come together seamlessly, and most of the time, they won't. Why? Because like building a muscle, you're building strength. If we look at this strictly from a physical fitness perspective, as you work out, you are actually stressing the muscles because that's how you grow them. You are pushing so hard that you are literally breaking the fiber within them. You are lifting 'til failure. It's the stress that grows the muscles. Stress is good (take note of that).

Now, to maximize the growth of our muscles, it's not just in stressing them but also in resting them, and we'll talk about that more in the next chapter, *Learning to Acclimate,* but there's no point in resting them if you're not even working them. When you work your muscles to the point of failure, then give them the time and attention they need to rest, recover, and heal, you actually strengthen them and prepare them for the next level of stress, I mean, success. The same is true for you. Stress will be par for the course. You can't resist it or run from it. You need to stop focusing so much on "how much you don't like stress" and start focusing on how you can maximize your recovery time so you can bounce back and be all you need to be for your life.

In real time, this is how this works: let's say you have a dream to be more patient. Do you think you are gifted with perfect circumstances that magically allow you to be more patient because everything is working out exactly how you planned? No way, man. You are likely presented with chaos. Why? Because patience isn't just given to us, it's developed in hard, trying scenarios. Patience is developed when we don't get our way, when things don't happen in the time we think they should, or when we have a challenging child to raise or a staff member to interact with. *That* develops true patience when we stand up against the chaos around us and aren't moved by the pressure and stress of it all but rather, lean in and build patience.

Another example is when we pray for more passionate relationships in our life. Do you think we suddenly are greeted by the most fantastic, perfectly passionate people to do life with? NO! We are greeted with the *opportunity* to build our passion. We are greeted with pressure. We may even find that the people who come into our lives have no passion, so we can learn how to "fan the flame." It may mean we have to cut out all the noise and the distractions to find our true passion. It may mean that we have to deal with our apathy and the reasons we aren't living passionately. You aren't just born with passion; it's built over time and with enough circumstances that give it the chance to grow.

If you dream of being a singer, a writer, or an activist of some sort, do you think that everything is going to come together exactly as you think it should? No! It's likely your journey to finding your tune, writing your words, or finding and fighting against an injustice is going to be hard, trying, and pressurized. It's going to cause you to lean in, push yourself, and consciously quiet the distractions around you. It's a good thing because anyone who has manifested this type of dream as a singer, writer, or activist recognizes how hard, draining, and emotional the business can be, so quite honestly, the strength, stamina, and muscle gained along the way is needed for the destination. This is the tool that helps you recognize that it's not just about the destination; it's about the strength developed along the way because if you can't manage the pressure and the stress of *obtaining* your dreams, how in the world are you going to be able to *sustain* them?

Regardless of your dream, it is within you to make you a stronger, better version of you. So yep, that means it's gonna suck some days. Yes, you are going to want to give up. Yep, you are going to doubt yourself; you're going to feel very vulnerable. You are going to look around at what everyone else is doing, and you're going to feel behind the eight ball. You are going to second-guess yourself and your decisions. BUT. Do. Not. Stop. Moving. Forward. Do another push-up. The end result is far worth the current stresses and pressure.

When you have hard conversations, when you want to go back to old habits and routines, when you don't want to make the call and the phone weighs a million pounds, when you'd rather sleep in, and when anger feels easier—remember that whatever situation you're in, it's developing strength within you. We need you not just to be a "skinny" believer, but a believer with muscles.

Now, let me also be clear that this kind of strength is much meatier than straight-up willpower, and I think if we're not careful, we will automatically cling to doing things in our own strength and understanding. Remember, manifesting your dreams is past the zone of understanding and also past the zone of your own strength (including willpower). Too often, we begin to carry the load, the pressure, and the stress all on our own, which is why we're exhausted and burnt out. You must recognize that, yes, God did build you to handle anything that comes your way, but not on your own accord. He doesn't say you can do everything on your own. What does the Bible say? "For I can do **everything** *through Christ, who gives me strength*" (Philippians 4:13, New Living Translation [emphasis mine]). "But the Lord stood at my side and gave me strength" (2 Timothy 4:17). "My grace is sufficient for you, for my power is made perfect in weakness" (2 Corinthians 12:9). Why are we given so many reminders? It was probably because God knew that life would require strength and that there would be a fine line between us developing our own strength and actually inviting Him to empower us so we could go beyond our own ability. Sure, you can lift 'til failure on your own but believe me, this process will be bigger than you and require more than just your own strength. Yes, use your strength, take ownership of how much more you really can do, but make sure in those moments of failure that you call upon the power of God who can do so much more than you *think* you can do.

May I remind you that the next time you're at the gym, doing one more push-up, even when you *think* you can't, is going to make you stronger. Even when you don't want to, the process of weight training will benefit you. Lifting 'til failure on this journey to manifesting your dreams, believe me, is going to make you better. Anything that can make us stronger, better people always gives us the opportunity to become more joyful in the journey. Hebrews says, "For the joy set before him he endured the cross" (Hebrews 12:2). As you can imagine, that process was not easy for Jesus, nor was it fun. So, why joy? How was there *joy set before him*? I think it's because Jesus knew the outcome. He knew that the prize far exceeded the pain. He knew that the manifestation of his dream far outweighed the temporary agony he had to endure (or for us, our lack of comfort). I think that Jesus understood the principle of the juxtaposition and knew that despite His reality, the pressure of the "push-ups" was going to give Him lasting significance.

Do you know the phrase, "The joy is in the journey?" This is exactly what it means. It's about the recognition of the process itself, not just the end destination, and realizing that the journey exists for your own benefit. It's about developing your belief (which we will do in Chapters 7 and 8). It's about finding your conviction (which we will do in Chapter 9) and learning how to stand against the things that are out of alignment (which we will do in Chapter 10). It's about getting you to look at your reality for what it is—no matter how sobering or ridiculous it may be—and establishing the courage and audacity to create something new and, yes, unfamiliar (which we will do in Chapter 11 and 12). It's about getting you to turn inward, so you can realize that the true power comes from within, God in you. Dreaming is designed to develop every part of you, so when the day comes and you accomplish those dreams, you also have the emotional, mental, spiritual, and financial fortitude not just to obtain what is important to you but also to have the skills, wisdom, and power (the muscles) to *sustain* what you've achieved.

Once you recognize and use this tool, you can then begin the climb. And yes, I did say climb!

Your DREAMS are not designed to keep you skinny, they're designed to help you build strength.

CHAPTER 5

Learning to Acclimate— Getting Comfortable in the Uncomfortable

THE FIRST TWO TOOLS IN YOUR TOOLBOX of creating awareness— identifying the juxtaposition and lifting 'til failure—are designed to help you *obtain* your dreams. The next two tools are designed to help you *sustain* your dreams as you move toward and even begin manifesting them.

The first tool to help you sustain your dreams is learning to **acclimate**.

Most are familiar with this concept as it pertains to climbing, an analogy we will use throughout this chapter. It's also very relevant to your own growth journey because as you grow, evolve, and gain greater awareness in all areas of life, you have to realize that there is an acclimation process that needs to happen; you'll literally need to let yourself grow accustomed to a new way of doing things. What got you to where you are won't get you to where you're going which means, you're going to have to do something totally different, and you're likely going to have to learn something totally new. Just like a climber climbing a mountain must enter new climate conditions, so too will you enter new environments, new lessons, and new conditions. In order to do that well, I am suggesting that you're going to need this tool of acclimating to sustain your growth.

You'll find that dreaming opens you up to states of awareness that can feel like a lot at first. It can be very deep. It can feel like opening up a can of worms, and it will absolutely feel uncomfortable. Most of us admit we don't like being uncomfortable so this can feel rather exposing. It feels exposing because it often requires that you face the things you've run from for years. It also causes you to realign with yourself, which can feel awkward at first because you begin to realize how out of alignment you've been, and like an adjustment at the chiropractor, it hurts and takes time to get back on track. It's also a bit scary and out of body to imagine our future because, for most, we can measure what we'll lose, but we can't understand what we'll gain.

Though learning, growing, evolving, and becoming who you are designed to be versus what everyone else thinks you should be *sounds good* and *is* good, still, of course, the process does take an emotional toll, no doubt, and can stimulate some insecurities, leave you feeling overwhelmed, alone, and even judged. For those courageous enough to take it on, it is important to recognize there is an art to obtaining *and* sustaining this level of growth without quitting or sabotaging your efforts. Ultimately, we have to learn how to apply this tool so we can use it because it's not a matter of *if* we will feel uncomfortable but *when*. So instead of avoiding the discomfort, I am giving you the chance to sit with it and move through it with more grace because the only way out is through.

So as you begin to move toward change, once things get uncomfortable, once movement begins to happen, how do you stick with it? How do you ensure you sustain it?

You acclimate.

To make this concept easier to digest, so you'll actually use it, I'm going to use the analogy of climbing Mt. Everest and relate it to your own dreaming journey. Why Mt. Everest? Well, considering it is the highest peak in the world and is known as an epitome of beauty, it represents true actualization, which is also the highest peak of awareness. It's the greatest gift we could work toward in this lifetime.

The Climb

Mt. Everest is just over 29,000 feet high, and only half who attempt to summit actually do. Although there are many different routes to the summit of Everest, most climb it one of two routes, the Southeast Ridge or the North Ridge. The ascent up contains a 19,685-foot altitude change and, on average, takes forty-sixty days to fully summit. Most climbers, once fully summited, can only withstand staying at the peak for fifteen minutes until their oxygen levels and body strength run out, and they are forced to begin their descent. It requires an insane amount of dedication and intensive training, as you can imagine.

For me, the most interesting thing about the journey to the summit is the acclimation process. Climbers, though maybe obvious, don't go straight to the summit of Mt. Everest. They have to stop at multiple camps along the way, with the goal of acclimating at each camp. Interestingly, they actually will go *past* each camp before coming back down to settle in. Why? Because they have to acclimate. To keep it simple, climbers climb past each camp to push their limits and prepare their lungs and body for what they're going to encounter next. That extra push is a struggle, it can also be a bit euphoric, out of body, and can even create mental blackouts for people. More than anything it is designed to *begin working those muscles within them in preparation for what's to come.* Climbers then come back down to each camp for recovery purposes. "Climb high, sleep low," they call it.

This is so important to maintain performance and to build strength for what's to come. If climbers move onto the next camp before they've undergone the process of acclimating, they could burn out or get really hurt, resulting in death. If they fail to acclimatize well lower down, they will struggle higher up, so it's extremely important for them to get the most out of their recovery time, which could include sleeping, eating appropriate food, supplemental oxygen, and dropping weight. A lot of this has to do with each climber's personal physiology. They must listen to their body and remain flexible with their acclimatization schedule to ensure that they are adjusting and not wearing themselves out.

Many people think you build the most muscle when you're working out, but you actually gain the most amount of success in your recovery time. That's why people who work out too much or don't take their recovery process seriously do more long-term damage than good. If you kept working out day after day after day, with little to no rest, it would eventually take a toll on your body. It wouldn't be sustainable. Equally so, the climb up Everest also requires active rest and for every 2,000 feet of climb (above 8,000 feet), climbers stay for a day or two of rest.

There are so many principles in climbing Everest that parallel your dreaming journey. Let's take a look at some of these parallel principles and how they apply.

Mt. Everest is the highest peak in the world you can summit.

The achievement of our dreams, heaven on earth, is the highest peak we can summit in our lives. It is purpose realized. It's one thing to *have* purpose, which we all do, but it's another to *realize* it. Abraham Maslow, an American psychologist best known for creating Maslow's hierarchy, called this *self-actualization*. He defined it as the realization and fulfillment of one's talents and potential. The hierarchy is a "triangle of human needs," which Maslow charted in 1943 as a set of important requirements for an individual to understand to achieve higher levels of development and self-actualization in life. Self-actualization is the highest level of psychological development after basic and esteem needs have been fulfilled.

The levels of hierarchy start with our basic physiological and safety needs—air, food, water, shelter, clothing, sex, sleep, and protection. Maslow then puts love and belonging (esteem needs)—dignity, accomplishments, and reputation, in the middle of the pyramid. These are all known as deficiency needs, which means once we achieve them, we don't need *more* of them to be happier and more fulfilled. Self-actualization—realizing personal potential, self-fulfillment, and peak experiences, are at the very top. These are known as growth needs. Too many of us only set our eyes and attention on deficiency-based needs, which is why we never summit our own Everest in life. However, just like climbing Everest, the point is to summit. The point is to bring your dreams to life. The way that we do that is by being cognizant of our deficiency needs while learning how to make decisions from our growth needs—a much higher perspective.

Mt. Everest takes rigorous training and preparation.

So does the fulfillment of your dreams. Whether you feel like it or not, you have been preparing your whole life for your dreams. Everything (and I do mean *everything*) has happened for a reason and has positioned you for everything that is still to come. Your dreams, like climbing Everest, are no easy undertaking and will require *continuous* training and preparation.

There are multiple routes to the top of Mt. Everest.

Believe it or not, there is no one way to accomplish your dreams. You do have choices, you do have options, and how you summit is completely up to you. Just because things don't go as planned or you experience a delay, setback, failure, or any other obstacle doesn't mean you can't reroute or pick another course. You can always shift your direction and still end up where we want to be. I think we often forget that God wants our dreams even more than we do, and even as we set out on a plan, thinking we know what we're doing, God knows even more. As it's written, "We can make our plans, but the Lord determines our steps" (Proverbs 16:9, NLT). Make plans, yes. Choose consciously, engage wisely in your route, yes, but then recognize that God is bigger than all of it and will guide and secure your steps as you go, even if you are rerouted.

Mt. Everest requires climbers to stop at multiple camps along the way so climbers can acclimate, adjust, and prepare for the climb's next phase.

This is probably the one we overlook the most, but it is just as necessary in our own lives. Do you recall those times in your life where you have undergone a huge amount of change, or even accomplish a goal, but then all of a sudden, you self-sabotage your own progress? What about those times when you hit some amazing goals and accomplish some amazing feats, but then, for whatever reason, you can't seem to sustain your progress? Or, you quit a habit only to pick it back up again? This is because, unlike Everest climbers, you aren't acclimating. You're expanding your capacity, and the expansion is too fast for you to keep up with it because even though things on the outside are changing, you aren't changing on the inside. Therefore, you can't sustain the "altitude change" of life. You must acclimate in each season of your life in order to sustain continual progress and growth.

Consider the story of David and Goliath. We all love the triumphant ending of David killing the giant, but David didn't just wake up one day and slay the giant. Prior to his victory, David's faith in God grew because of his experiences protecting his sheep from daily predators—coyotes, wolves, bears, and lions—so when the day came to fight Goliath, he was ready and victory was inevitable because he had been acclimating his fear and his faith along the way.

Climbers release gear at every camp.

At each new camp, climbers aren't gearing up but rather *letting go* of gear because it increases their ability to progress. Too much baggage on an already slippery slope and they won't sustain the journey. Like these climbers, you must be more conscious of what you're taking with you on your journey because it's likely that what got you to where you are won't take you to where you've never been. For you and I, that means we need to downsize the weight that doesn't serve us, be it literal, emotional, mental, relational, or physical. It could be letting go of habits, patterns, beliefs, relationships, routines, what you eat or drink, and even how you treat yourself. If you keep trying to take with you all the things that got you to where you are, you won't free yourself to climb toward all that's awaiting you.

This is another principle that I learned well when we sold everything in 2018 and began our full-time RV travels. I can remember the day that we opened our front door for what we called our "Living Estate Sale," where we sold everything at a discounted rate, only to be bombarded by people for two hours until literally everything we owned was gone. As one might imagine, it was freeing and crazy vulnerable all at the same time. I'd like to pretend that I didn't find my identity or comfort in the stuff I had accumulated but, on that day, it was very obvious that I had.

I have learned firsthand that manifesting your dreams is less about acquiring and achieving more, but rather, what you are willing to let go of to go where you've never gone. There's a reason Jesus says, "Sell everything … Then come, follow me" (Mark 10:21). Why? Because Jesus understood that where your treasure is, there your heart will be also. If your heart is not grounded in the dreams connected to the heart of God, you will get distracted, weighed down, and burdened by all the unnecessary stuff. It's not that God doesn't want you to live in abundance and to have the most beautiful, finest things in life; it's that he doesn't want those things to have you. By acknowledging and letting go of your attachment to the stuff, to the distractions, habits, unhealthy behaviors, and to the things that are taking you away from the real manifestations of the dreams inside of you, you are making your path easier and your burdens lighter, so you can run the race set out before you.

Amazing parallels.

As you learn and grow, you will be exposed to new truths, options, ideas, and strategies that emotionally, mentally, financially, and spiritually stretch you. It's a new condition. It's new territory you've never experienced or been exposed to before, so it's only natural for your need to acclimate. In order to stretch your capacity and to endure the stress (because, as we talked about in the last chapter, stress is a part of life) you have to understand how to acclimate and when to give yourself time for recovery, to adjust to new conditions. That's why after having a hard conversation, an intense workout, having a baby, moving across the country, trying something new that challenges you or you've never done before, watching a child go off to college, or even after attending a class or business meeting you can feel exhausted. It's because you are pushing your limits of understanding, physical, and mental capabilities. That is okay; it's a good thing. That's where you want to be! However, you want to ensure you don't keep pushing and that you take some time to acclimate, or it's likely it won't last. It's why we see people become famous only to sabotage their success or win the lottery to go bankrupt three years later. Why? Because they can't *sustain* what they've just *obtained*. They climbed past "camp two," went straight to "camp three," and expected to be fine. It doesn't work that way.

Climbers on Everest strategically acclimate for a reason and though they may just want to cruise past each camp, it will never serve them because they won't be able to sustain the entire climb. They sleep, eat, and let go of gear. For you and me, in our day to day life, acclimating may look like additional sleep, talking with our counselor, meditating and praying, journaling, cleansing, honoring the Sabbath day as a holy day of rest, or simply going on a walk to ensure we are clearing our heads so our hearts can embrace the exposure to something new. But most of us don't do that. We just keep going, keep pushing, or keep driving toward another goal with no acknowledgment of the one we just accomplished. We take another pill, drink another glass of wine, pretending it didn't jar our current understanding, and then we wonder why we aren't executing at our highest levels. We are human y'all, and sure, some may be able to sustain more change than others, but all of us have our limits, so this theory is designed to assist you in your growth.

While manifesting your dreams, you will have days that you will feel doubt, you won't feel equipped to handle or manage all that your heart wants to do, and you're going to have to acknowledge that you've hit a threshold, which is par for the course. It's a sign to acclimate. If you don't, you run the risk of not being able to sustain the growth or, heaven forbid, like Everest, you fall into the 50 percent who don't summit because you're not taking care of yourself. By acclimating, you will grow your capacity. Grow your capacity, and just like the climbers, you will summit. I promise.

As you take these steps toward your own summit of understanding, be mindful of the signs, be mindful of not pushing yourself so hard that you can't sustain your progress, take the "camp" to recover as needed, and acclimate as you go. When you feel emotionally flustered and physically drained, when you start to lack clarity, when fear, doubt, and worry creep in, when hard conversations start to shut you down, when things aren't aligning, or when you feel insecure in your skill level or understanding, just be mindful of where you are. Acclimate. Catch up with where you are. Take care of yourself in preparation for where you're going.

As you begin to move forward in the next chapters of this book, from opening awareness to building belief to taking action, I want you to envision that you're entering a new "camps." Like each level of the dreaming process, each "camp" has a variety of climate changes, challenges, *and* uncertainties. Here I do my best to describe them in a way that shows the parallels between "camps."

Let's take a peak ☺.

Camp 1

Creating Awareness (something you've done in these first couple chapters):

On Mt. Everest, the territory right out of the gate is extremely dangerous for any climber and needs a lot of care and attention. Climbers can expect shifting and falling ice, avalanches, crackling sounds, crunching, and even shifting crevices beneath them. As a climber, you can imagine how much this will wake you up! "Ready or not!" This part requires the climber to begin paying serious attention to what's going on around them. It just got real.

For you, this phase is very similar, and instead of camp 1, we'll call it *Creating Awareness.* This is the phase when you are taking in *tons* of information. New knowledge, insights, and perspectives are flying at you. You begin to connect the dots in your life. You start scratching the surface of the things you've been avoiding, and you can feel like there is this cracking and crunching of thoughts, ideas, and states of awareness beginning to happen. Movement is happening, change is starting to take place, and it requires you to start paying attention to what's going on within you, maybe at a level that you never have before. You begin to feel emotions you've never felt before, begin to think thoughts you've never thought before, and in many ways, you begin to question everything to find your real truth. The good news is that this phase, though uncomfortable, gets you awake and alert. You are now paying attention.

This first phase of creating awareness is awesome in that yes, you are alive, alert, and wide-awake but you can also feel completely overwhelmed by a lack of cognitive understanding. This can leave you feeling rather insecure because of your lack of automatic knowledge or "know-how." You have to understand that when you climb to new levels of awareness and understanding, it's like learning a new skill. If we're honest, we all experience a wide variety of emotions at different stages of the learning process. We may not realize how much we need to learn to progress to the next level. Once we start to weigh in on all that we don't know and all that we have yet to learn, we can become easily disheartened, insecure, and even want to give up. Being able to recognize this and how to actually manage ourselves and our emotions are key.

Noel Burch, an employee with Gordon Training International, called these levels of learning the Conscious Competency Ladder. He developed this ladder of learning in the 1970s, and it highlights two factors that affect our thinking as we learn something new: consciousness (awareness) and skill level (competency). According to this model, we move through different levels of awareness and competency as we learn and grow, starting with **Unconscious Incompetency**—you don't know what you don't know, and you are unaware that you are unaware. Here, it's like being asleep to your life. This is the "ignorance is bliss" phase.

Next, we move into **Conscious Incompetency**—which is like our first camp. This is where you begin to wake up. I had one coaching student who said, "I didn't even know that I had fallen asleep to my life. Now what?" Here, you are aware enough to know that you are stuck but not aware enough to know how to get unstuck. You begin to wake up to states of awareness that you didn't even recognize before and become more conscious that you know you need to change, but you feel inept in understanding how to make a change. The fact that your levels of actual competency are super low makes this part unusually hard. Typically this is when we feel inadequate and experience higher levels of self-doubt, which is why we give up. Nobody likes to be *consciously* not good at something. If you stick with it, though, you will progress, I promise. You *will* gain competency, you will gain skill, but you're going to have to "climb for it." If you give up or go back, you are only going back to an unconscious state of incompetency, which, in my opinion, is much worse! Keep going! In the midst of the cracks and crevices and triggers, keep going.

Camp 2

Building Belief (something you'll do in the next section):

On Everest, this is the long trek for the climbers that feels hard enough to make them push but not so hard they can't sustain the ascent. The trickiest part here, believe it or not, is the heat! Because there is so little wind and climbers are faced with intense direct sunlight, it gets hot. They're also into the trek far enough that it starts to feel like an eternity. They can no longer see the bottom, the top is nowhere in sight, and it feels as though it's the great hallway of in between.

For you, in your journey, this is the phase in which you are *building belief*. In anthropology, the study of humans and human behavior, this is called liminal space, which can be described as the time in between what was and what's next.

This is a concept that changed my life. Years ago, I can remember sitting with a good friend, eating Thai food, and telling her of my odd state of being. "I just feel so out of body," I can remember telling her. "It's like I'm physically here, but I don't feel here. My mind and body feel numb. Some days I'm on top of the world, and some days, I just want to crawl back into bed. I feel like I'm floating, then I feel like I'm really heavy. My mind has a million thoughts and then absolutely none. What's wrong with me?!" She graciously looked up from her noodle bowl, and with so much love and gratitude, said, "You're in liminal space."

Like climbing Everest, liminal space is very much like the great hallway of in between. It's where you've started the process of letting go of one thing but not yet grabbed onto another. It's a place of transition and where all the transformation takes place because you are breaking old habits and beginning the process of establishing new ones. But let's be honest, that's difficult. Letting go of the things that we know and understand, letting go of our norm, and letting go of familiar things (even if they don't serve us) can feel like a lot. This is why many people say they want to change, but few actually do.

This phase can feel like you're on a roller coaster of emotions where one day you're on top of the world, but the next, not so much. You may even feel a bit bipolar, crazy, or confused. You may be physically present but not have words. You may feel a bit blank, even emotionless. Others attest to feeling more emotional than usual but don't have any real reason as to why. Some days the trust and faith walk feels good and other days you're like, dang, this sucks. For most, this place is quiet—really, really quiet. And truth be told, we're not used to quiet. It's as though we've "cleaned house" only to find deep stillness.

Welcome to liminal space. You are in the in between, between what was and what's next, between consciously incompetent and consciously competent.

Though this phase is challenging and you will feel the discomfort of waiting and the pressure of not knowing at an automatic cognitive level, it's the best, juiciest, and most necessary phase because are *building new belief*, and even though you can't see it, it's happening. If you can learn to be patient in this belief-building phase, in this quiet place, your life will transform. The Bible says, "Be still, and know that I am God" (Psalm 46:10). Believe it or not, this is what strengthens your connection to yourself and to Him. This is where you learn the power of being still. This is where you learn the power of trust, letting go, and leaning into Him in ways you didn't even know you weren't before.

Camp 3

Creation Zone (something you'll do in the final two chapters):

This is where the Everest climbers are trekking up some serious slopes. Heart rates are at an all-time high. Climbers literally begin to focus on one foot in front of the other because that's all they can do. They're feeling the pain of the physical demands, and therefore, they are forced to begin this journey of "going in." They're far beyond the self-talk game, and in fact, most don't even recognize their thoughts because this is the endurance zone. Though painstakingly challenging, it's a beautiful thing because, as a climber, your mind begins to shut off and your body begins to take over. If you're in your head, you're dead.

In real life, this is the *creation zone*, baby! You have let go of the old and you've grabbed onto the new, which means you're now consciously choosing a different way to live—your thoughts, habits, actions, everything. You are past thinking, and instead, you are in your heart. In this phase, you are dreaming. You are brainstorming. You are researching. You are writing, drawing, planning, preparing, and starting to put pieces together. Emotionally, you are dealing with the pain by doing something with it. Instead of hiding from it, you are creating with it. You're finding a rhythm. You're finding your greatest commitments and convictions, and you're learning to lean in even when you used to lean out. Your life is moving in a new direction.

This is the **Conscious Competency** phase. Here your doubt subsides and your confidence often grows because you are conscious of your own levels of competency. However, it still requires a ton of focus, mental effort, and attention. This phase is like driving home a new way where you are no longer dependent on MapQuest to find your way home like you once were, but you're still paying close attention to where you're going because it's not yet automatic, and you could easily get lost if you get side-tracked. This is a sweet zone to be in because here, you are laser-focused on the dreams at hand, which normally means whatever you're doing gets all of you, completely engaged, no multi-tasking allowed! This will force you to limit all other distractions and go all in.

Camp 4

Dreaming into Doing:

For climbers on Mt. Everest, this is probably the most treacherous part and yet, the most revealing because they are pushing their limits in ways they only thought about. Though they've practiced and trained for this moment, it is nothing in comparison to the real deal. Climbers are tired; they've been climbing for weeks now, the path itself is treacherous, plus they're pushing for the summit. Their brain shut off days ago, their senses are even a bit dulled, there's little to no chatter going on, and all they can do is keep going because even though it's hard, moving forward is easier than going back. They've got a single, laser focus—summit.

This phase is my favorite because here, your faith grows wings, and you begin to fly. This is when you, along with your dreams, begin to actualize. This is the *execution zone*, when we "act our way to a new way of thinking." This is where you have officially transitioned from your heart into full-blown motion. You're connecting your dreams and plans with real activity. At this phase, you are no longer thinking about doing it, talking about doing it, or even brainstorming on how to do it; you are doing it. You're not listening to the chatter of the brain because there is none. You do not need to be convinced, you already are, and you are just *doing it*. You're in it, and you've completely lost yourself to the journey. Here you live on faith, instinct, and intuition (a place we don't live from enough). You'll find yourself saying things like "I don't know how, but we'll figure it out as we go" because you know, you can't turn back now and you know that God is with you, so who could be against you? Just like climbing Everest, you stay focused on the prize because if you look down, you'll fall; if you look up too much, you'll freak out; if you look too much to the side, you'll get dizzy. You just put your head down, and you climb! You don't have time to judge your progress or to compare your journey to someone else's because you're 100 percent committed to your climb.

This is the **Unconscious Competency** phase. This is where the things that you've learned now become automatic, and you don't have to give any more conscious thought to what you're doing because it's become so natural. This means your habits, patterns, and routines have transformed, and just like when you started, you don't have to give a whole lot of concentrated thought to what you're doing because you're just doing it. It no longer feels forced. Your mind chatter doesn't fight with you anymore because it finally feels comfortable in what it's doing, and you've moved into a familiar zone, so there's less resistance from yourself. It's a cool spot to be!

Summit
Dreams Actualized:

BOOM, and just like that, a climber's dream—they're on top of Mt. Everest! The views are epic. It's everything they dreamed of and more. The accomplishment is insane. It's just the most beautiful moment ever!

The same goes for you. You're on top of your mountain. You've actualized your dreams. You feel in tune, accomplished, proud, excited, tired, and over-whelmed with emotion all at the same time! This is one of those waypoints where you've actually manifested a dream. You see how your hard work has paid off, and you get to enjoy the fruits of your labor. It's a beautiful thing. Unlike standing at the summit of Everest, this phase is longer than fifteen minutes and is absolutely something to be enjoyed, but at some point in time, just like the climbers on Mt. Everest, life must continue. We must turn the page to the next chapter in our life, which means, what goes up, must come down. But enjoy the views, the hope it brings, the confidence it builds, and, just like on Everest, prepare for the descent.

The Descent
Life:

For climbers, the descent can be just as physically demanding as the ascent, and truth be told, climbers spend as much, if not more, time going down the mountain as they do going up. It's a different mode than climbing up, obviously, but requires tons of energy, nonetheless. It's about patience, perseverance, sustainability, and focus. Climbers don't want to go down too fast, nor do they want to go down too slowly. They have to be extremely careful, because though they experienced euphoria at the summit, they are physically exhausted at this point and likely to get hurt if they're not paying attention.

The same goes for you. Just as you have the pressure of the ascent (journey) and the beauty at the top (accomplishment), you also endure the descents of life, the twists and turns, the ups and downs, but, unlike Everest, there is no timeline. These are what are called seasons in life. Because you're never really "there," nor ever really done until that last breath of air is breathed, just like growing accustomed to all the ascents and summits, you, too, must become comfortable in the descents of life. Every part of your journey has an impact on who you're becoming, and if you approach this consciously and with sincere trust in yourself and God's leading, it will make you better with every step. If you allow every moment to be exactly what it needs to be, you will enjoy the climb and the descent just as much as the summit because it all leads into the next chapters of life. The peaks wouldn't be as good if you didn't live through the valleys, and the valleys wouldn't be as sustainable without the amazing peaks. Therefore, your awareness and maturity start to recognize the beauty and importance of all of it, not judging or resisting any of it.

If nothing else, may you see that each step in this dreaming journey will require new phases of consciousness that are necessary for your soul. Every step along the way—every camp—is designed to make you stronger and to support you in seeing more clearly. Each phase lasts for however long it needs to. Each phase is relevant and extremely necessary as you grow in consciousness and competency, aiding in the development of your skills and the accomplishment of your dreams. Who you are at the top of Everest—the manifestation of your dreams—is earned through every step along the way. Yes, getting to the top of these mountains is a huge part of it, but who you become along the way is priceless.

Be prepared. Just like climbing Mt. Everest, it'd be silly not to understand these phases of dreaming. As mentioned, it's *not* for the faint of heart; it's for the courageous and prepared. Recognize when you're self-sabotaging or when you need to be *letting go* of something so you can continue your climb.

Recognize when it's time for active rest, recognize what your mind, body, and soul are all telling you, and recognize the times when you need to shut off the brain and just get 'er done.

More than anything, I encourage you to acclimate as we move through this work. You are going to gain awarenesses that will need to be processed. Do not rush through this just to check it off the list. Allow your internal shift and external shift to be in alignment with each other so you can sustain what you obtain. Your vision and dreams will take maintenance, and it will take a sort of strength that is only grown on the journey. It can't be earned just by getting to the top. It's earned in the darkest valleys as well as in the "in betweens," during the good times and the hard, so please be sure to take care of yourself.

Alrighty climbers, by now, you get the gist. This isn't going to be easy but, now that you understand the climb ahead, it's sure to be a bit more simple. Now that you're aware, let's build some belief.

You're "ascent"
to the top of your
DREAMS is about
your willingness to let
go of the things that
no longer serve you
so you can go where
you've never gone.

SECTION 2

BUILDING YOUR BELIEF

CHAPTER 6

Check Your Thoughts— Your First Step Toward Mastering Your Mind

OUR FOURTH AND FINAL TOOL is one you will use on a daily basis and is particularly practical as you begin your journey of building belief. It's called **mastering your mind**.

The Bible says, "Do not conform to the pattern of this world, but be transformed by the renewing of your mind. Then you will be able to test and approve what God's will is—his good, pleasing and perfect will" (Romans 12:2). I'm going to teach you how to do exactly that.

If you recall, way back in Chapter 2, I spoke about the difference between your heart and your head. I shared with you that one of the reasons dreaming is so powerful is because it's connected to your heart space, not your head, and we spent a good amount of time talking about what it means to live from your heart, your *whole* heart. Now, let's talk about what I mean when I say, "head."

Your "head" is the house for your mind and your brain. Though there is so much more going on between your two ears, for the sake of simplifying it, we are going to focus in on these two components. In essence, at an elementary level, your mind is your thoughts, and your brain is the wiring system to confirm whether or not your thoughts as true or false. We'll start with your brain first.

Your brain, which is the physical part of your "head," works like a computer. It processes the information it receives from your senses, and it sends those messages back to the body. It controls and coordinates your actions and reactions and is designed to keep you safe. It's wired to help you *not* die. It survives by keeping you where you are. That's its job. It's built to help you *survive* by means of intellectually understanding, measuring, comprehending, remembering, compartmentalizing, judging, and planning. Why does it do that? To protect itself and, ultimately, keep you safe. Because survival is the basis and the premise for existence, we should use the brain that way, very intentionally in that manner, as a checks and balance system. Period.

Now, let's look at your mind, the nonphysical part of your "head" where your thoughts reside. If your brain is the meat of the sandwich, your mind and thoughts are the bread. In essence, how they work together is very simple and yet so complex! Your mind actually teaches your brain what to think because with every experience, you create a thought (both conscious and unconscious) and those thoughts trigger thousands of neurons in your brain. It's when you think about those thoughts over and over again that your brain learns to trigger those same neurons over and over again, really as a way to conserve energy by creating short cuts, which means you've actually taught yourself how to think, without thinking about it. Ultimately, it's the powers of your mind that build your brain, and it's your brain's neural patterns that create and reinforce your thoughts. But this is just the beginning.

According to cognitive behavioral therapy, **every thought creates an emotion**, which means your emotions don't just show up on the scenes. You don't wake up *feeling* insecure, fearful, angry, or even happy, peaceful, or excited. "That's just the way I am" doesn't apply. *Every* emotion, whether good or bad, has been preceded by a thought. Every. Single. Time. You're not sad "just because." You're not mad "just because." You're not even happy "just because." Something else is creating your positive and negative emotions. What is it? Ten out of ten times, you will find a thought.

"I am not good enough" (thought), and BOOM, hopelessness (emotion) sets in.

"No one supports me" (thought), and BOOM, anger (emotion) sets in.

"I don't know what I want" (thought), and BOOM, anxiety (emotion) sets in.

"What will people think of me?" (thought), and BOOM, fear (emotion) sets in.

The same is true on the other spectrum of thought processes.

"God's got my back, and I am more than a conqueror" (thought), and BOOM, happiness (emotion) sets in.

"His grace is sufficient for me" (thought), and BOOM, hope (emotion) sets in.

"I may not know how, but I am going to figure it out" (thought), and trust (emotion) sets in!

"I am a child of God" (thought), and love (emotion) sets in.

Thoughts create emotions, so if we can establish early on that we are the creators of our emotions because we are the creators of our thoughts, then we can change our emotions by changing our thoughts. By changing our thoughts, we literally begin the process of rewiring our brain.

As it's written, "We demolish arguments and every pretension that sets itself up against the knowledge of God, and we take captive every thought to make it obedient to Christ" (2 Corinthians 10:5). It doesn't say take every emotion captive. It says, "take every thought captive." So if you want to feel loving, happy, and trusting, then what thought do you have to think? How about: *I am loved. I am fully supported. I am a child of God. I am an overcomer.* See what I mean? This is an extraordinary, powerful concept! This confirms that your head (mind and brain) is *not* where you will create your dreams from, but it will either support you or hinder you from the actual process of dreaming. If that head of yours is feeding into its own negative thoughts, you will be executing from a survival, primal state and *nothing* good, beautiful, or progressive comes from this place. But if you are consciously leading your own thoughts, taking every thought captive to make it obedient to Christ, and actively creating an environment in that head space of yours that is open, willing, curious, and unattached (which takes practice), then you will actually be in alignment with your heart and on the same team as your dreams.

This also indicates that your dreams are not your emotions or your feelings. Your heart is not your emotions. Your emotions and feelings are birthed from your thoughts, not your dreams. This means you can be *emotional* and not be in your heart. I've heard from many people who say, "I'm a heart person because I am a very emotional person," and I say with as much grace and love as possible that living from heart has nothing to do with being emotional! Emotions are just reactions from your thoughts, not your dreams.

How then do we take every thought captive? How do we make our thoughts obedient to Christ? This is something I heard all my life growing up but didn't understand or use until I started to check my thoughts and emotions at the door. This is the first step in mastering your mind.

When I say, check your thoughts and emotions at the door, I literally mean "check." I want you to start acknowledging everything you are thinking and everything you are feeling and then begin looking at all of it simply for what is—information. Nothing more and nothing less. Then, I want you to consider this analogy:

* *

> *Your thoughts and emotions are just information at the*
> *door of your understanding, and your home is your life.*
> *Your thoughts and emotions will always be gracious*
> *enough to knock, but ultimately, you get to decide if you are*
> *going to open the door to your home to let them in.*

* *

I admit, I never opened the door to my emotions. Knock, knock, knock they might, but no matter how hard or how many times they knocked, I did not let them in. Maybe you can relate. Emotions felt dangerous to me. I didn't like them because I couldn't control them. I found them to be a sign of weakness, so I lived much of my life without them, completely avoiding them. I unconsciously felt as though I couldn't afford to have them. By doing so, my emotions stacked up on the outside of my door until ultimately, they shattered my doorway. You see, avoiding our emotions doesn't make them go away; it only prolongs the inevitable. We're not supposed to ignore our emotions or our thoughts, nor are we to open up the door and let any and every emotion and thought come into our house *unchecked*. Instead, we should hear the knock, open the door, check (process) what we see and feel, and then decide if those emotions and thoughts are worthy enough to enter our home.

Beware of letting every thought take a seat in your home. When you have thoughts like, "I'm not enough," "I can't depend on anyone," and "I don't trust God" knock at your door and you welcome them in like it's some high school friend you're just catching up with, you're doing serious damage. No, no, no, NO! Wake-up call—this is not some good high school friend that deserves a seat in your home. This is a bad friend who's taken a seat on your couch and is speaking nothing but death over you. And you're allowing it. The same is true with your emotions. Fear, doubt, and anxiety knock on your door, and you just welcome them in like they're the guests of honor. "Take a seat, make yourself at home, and tell me all your woes!"

By mastering your mind, it will become your goal to check every thought and emotion at the door, not ignore them, and not to just let them in. Instead, stand with them, process them, identify the thought pattern that created them, and consciously decide if they're worthy of taking a room within your home. You need to check them.

As cognitive behavioral therapy goes on to explain, every thought creates an emotion, and every emotion then leads to an action.

. . . .

Thoughts → Emotions → Action → Results

. . . .

For many of us, we feel angry and then often see ourselves as "an angry person" because we are making decisions from our anger. We think angry thoughts, feel angry emotions, and make angry decisions, which unconsciously implies, "I am an angry person." Here's some life-changing insight: you're not an angry person. You just *feel* angry. And guess what, that makes you human. Because emotions are information, this means you can *feel* angry, sad, or fearful without those feelings having anything to do with your truth. You can feel whatever you need to feel, and I do recommend feeling it all, hearing it all, and healing it all, but hear me when I say none of it defines you. If your emotions feel like they are defining you, it's because they've gone unchecked, and the problem with unchecked emotions is the tendency to give too much weight to them. We *feel* sad, so we must *be* a sad person. We *feel* angry so we must be an angry person. We begin to identify with our emotions instead of seeing them as just that, emotions (information).

Let's look at the impact of this in reverse order. Consider that today you are avoiding conflict, you're overweight, you're settling in your relationship or career, you're completely broke financially, or, on the opposite end of the spectrum, you're doing really well with your health and fitness, your love life is off-the-charts great, or your career is on an amazing path. Regardless of the results you're getting, they didn't just happen *to* you; they are a by-product of emotions that are locked and loaded with a thought. This means your results today have been built in thought from yesterday. If you didn't believe the thought, it wouldn't be so prominent in your life. If you believed or carried a thought that said that money was a blessing, you'd have more of it. If you believed or had a thought that said your body was the most important asset on the planet (God's holy temple), you would take care of it. If you believed or had a thought that you are worthy and deserving, a child of God, you would attract such things in your life. It doesn't mean all of it was easy or perfect or that bad things, circumstances, or things outside of your control wouldn't happen. But it does mean that you would approach life being much more unapologetic in your thought processes because you're actually grounded in the truth.

Pretty brilliant, huh?!

Hear your thoughts, stand with your emotions at the doorway of your home, and then check them both. If your thoughts are not serving you or giving you the emotions you want to have, perhaps it's time to give them up and consider a thought process that would actually serve you. Perhaps it's time to measure those thoughts against the very Word of God.

Give it a try:

What emotion do you *want* to feel most right now? Love? Trust? Happiness? Write it here:

_____

_____

_____

Okay, great. Now, what thought would you have to think in order to create that emotion? (Example: "There is more than enough." Or even as simple as "I am supported by the Lord my God.") Write your answer here:

_____

_____

_____

Now, taking your aligned thought and considering the emotion it creates (how it makes you feel), what actions would you take? What results would you create?

_____

_____

_____

Use the above exercise as many times as you need to direct your thoughts and emotions in a more progressive way on any given day. By consciously checking your thoughts and emotions at the doorway of your life, over time, you begin to do what I call "master your mind," something that is completely necessary in order to manifest your dreams. Mastering your mind helps you manifest your dreams because it is a tool that will help you hear what your heart has been saying all along by keeping your head in check.

That being said, no doubt about it, mastering your mind is definitely a brilliant tool and a way to start moving your thoughts in a new direction, but how many of you find yourself chanting, repeating morning mantras, and even doing a lot of praying, but your thought patterns just aren't changing? How many of you would even admit that you know God's Word, but it doesn't seem to be doing a whole lot in your life? Yeah, I've been there too. Again, I grew up knowing many scriptures and could spout them off to you without batting an eye, but why were they "not working?" Why did they seem power-less to me? Back to my earlier point, we know but we don't *know*.

This is because there is a difference between a thought and a belief. A thought can be fleeting, it comes and it goes. Then there's what I call a *super-charged thought*. A supercharged thought is one that has enough positive or negative impact on us that it becomes something that we think about (consciously and unconsciously) over and over and over again, therefore creating neural pathways in our brain, which creates a lens through which we view life, whether accurate or not. This is also called a belief. As you're about to learn, **our beliefs are the most profound, unchartered opportunity we have as people because it is our beliefs that are building our world.** If these beliefs are not in alignment with our dreams or what God's doing, it can create a lot of issues in our lives. It can also be extremely difficult to break the beliefs that don't serve us unless we shine the light of consciousness on them. Which is exactly what we're going to do next.

You can't be in your head and following your DREAMS at the same time because your head will not take you to where you've never been. That's for matters of the heart.

CHAPTER 7

Diving into Your Beliefs Part 1

Belief Formation and the Good Ol' Limiting Belief

ANYTHING WE CLAIM TO BE POSSIBLE or impossible *is*. How do I know that to be true? Well, if you look around, one person will say, "It's impossible to be a millionaire" when the fact is there are over 18.6 million in the United States alone. Someone else might have said that "running a 4.5 minute mile is impossible" until Roger Bannister proved it was possible in 1954. The bottom line is, it doesn't matter if all these stats are true or not, to the person who said it was "impossible," it was true, and to the person who said it was "possible," it was also true. Why? Because of the power of a belief!

What do our beliefs have to do with dreaming? Everything, because

93

what you believe impacts *everything* because *belief* shapes everything. It literally shapes your reality. That means whatever you have going on in your life *today* was birthed by a belief established *yesterday*, whether good, bad, or indifferent. You show me how you live, and I'll tell you what you believe.

This can often be where we get hung up when it comes time to dream because dreaming is about creating from a place of imagination and future. In contrast, most of our current beliefs are created unconsciously from our past experiences and interpretations of what's behind us, not what awaits us. Little did we know, we are living much of our current reality based upon the beliefs we created in our past, so our ability to override those old beliefs with new dreams, ideas, or even goals can be rather challenging. That's why we've got to understand how our beliefs are formed and the influence our beliefs are having on our dreams.

Take a look at what I call the Dream Tree, something we will reference throughout the rest of the book. Let's just say that if your life's results were the fruit on a tree, your beliefs would be the seed.

Everything is built from the seed. Just as a tree is built from its seed, *everything* in our lives is also built from our seeds (beliefs). Instead of teaching you better ways to chop away at your fruit (results), I'm going to show you how to identify what your seed says, so you can either water the tree better or completely uproot the tree and plant a different seed.

Pretend you're getting apples in your life today because you planted an apple seed years ago, but now you want oranges. What most of us do in life is spend way too much time whacking away at the apples. We feel good about ourselves as we cut away at all the apples until we realize that the growth coming back is not changing. We are still getting apples. So without giving it much thought, we go chopping away at our fruit, over and over, no longer focused on watering or growing more trees, but rather cutting off each and every apple that pops up, thinking we will cure the apple problem.

I hate to break it to you, but you will never get rid of your apples by cutting away at the fruit. They will only continue to grow back. You have to deal with the seed. The *only* way you go from having an apple tree to an orange tree is to uproot the entire apple tree, the root system and all, and replant it with an orange seed. We focus so much on what we see (our fruit, the results in our life) that we go from diet plan to diet plan, relationship to relationship, job to job, only to find that we are creating many of the same choices and habits over and over again. *Wherever you go, there you are* couldn't be more true. I am encouraging us to stop chopping away at the fruit and, for a minute or two or a hundred, to look at something much deeper so that we can stimulate much deeper change and growth. Let's stop trying to change habits, routines, and all the stuff on the outside. Instead, let's deal with our belief system on the inside. The bad news is that you're going to have to confront and deal with these core beliefs to change anything. The good news is if you want to change anything, and I do mean *anything*, you now know exactly where to begin: with your beliefs.

What are beliefs and how are they formed?

Beliefs are our acceptance of something as true. To my earlier point, they are thoughts that we think about over and over again that become a pattern in our thinking, to the point of unverifiable truth. They've even been described as the habits of the mind. Here's what I find to be fascinating about beliefs: Our beliefs are similar to memories, only they become our truths. They help us provide stability in our lives by compartmentalizing everything in order to make sense of the world, therefore allowing each of us to create our own interpretations so we can better understand everything that's happening around us. Our beliefs are like the positions we endorse or unconscious commitments we make because of the views and opinions that we have accumulated over time.

Our beliefs are the most profound, unchartered opportunity we have as people because it is our beliefs that are building our world.

We are spending so much time and energy trying to change our world from the outside in, when in fact, where we need to start is from the inside out. Our change needs to occur at our own belief level. Most of us know what other people are saying. We know what the news is saying, what our friends, siblings, and family members are saying. The problem is, we don't actually know what we're saying. It's not hard to identify what someone else believes, but we don't actually know what we believe, or worse than that, we don't know *why* we believe what we believe.

The worst thing we could do is to live blind to our own beliefs, not to know *why* we believe what we believe, to ignore our current beliefs, to pretend the ones we have don't influence us, or to try to force new ones when we really can't back them up. There is a process to this, and we're going to spend some time in this chapter unpacking where your current beliefs came from so you can decide how you want to address those and ultimately change them if they're no longer serving you.

Believe it or not, beliefs *are* formed. There has been a ton of research on belief formation, which ultimately proves that our beliefs don't just randomly show up on the scene of our lives. They do have a starting point, and they are developed over time. There are multiple influences that take place that curate and cultivate these beliefs and ultimately drive and influence our lives in every way. That means if we want to change anything in our life or our world, we need to start with our beliefs. We need to start with our seed.

Change the seed; change the fruit. Change your beliefs; change your world.

A changed world will come through changed beliefs.

Belief Formation

If we are going to do our part to get our lives back and build a world congruent with our dreams, we are going to have to begin the process of taking every thought captive to ensure it's serving us and the greater good. The good news is, in the last chapter, I taught you the first step in taking every thought captive by "checking it at the door." However, though it's *that* simple, it's surely not *that* easy.

As mentioned, though similar, your thoughts and beliefs are different, so let's ensure you are not confused. Your thoughts are actually the birthplace of your beliefs. A thought can come and go. You put no additional energy or emotion toward it unless you let it into your home. When you let unchecked thoughts come into your home, over time, they take a seat in your life, and when they've been sitting there long enough, you begin to believe them to be true. They become a part of your life and ultimately shape how you live, how you love, and how you view yourself and other people. They become beliefs. Here's how this works:

A belief first begins when an **EXPERIENCE** in time occurs. That experience, on paper, is not bad or good; it's just an experience. An experience only has meaning when we decide to give it meaning. *All meaning is in our mind. It's in our thoughts.*

For most, because we are trying to understand our experiences, especially those that are both painful and beautiful, we automatically give them meaning. We create **INTERPRETATIONS**. Another way to say this is we create *thought* processes around our experiences. We do this in order to stabilize a very unstable world. As people, we are wired for certain levels of certainty (some more than others), so when we experience something, whether positive or negative, we create interpretations—thought processes—because it gives us what appears to be a more concrete understanding of a circumstance or situation. Our interpretations are the *meaning* behind the experience.

Once we have created an interpretation of an experience to compartmentalize what just happened, we begin doing our due diligence to confirm our suspicion. We are unconsciously thinking, "Is this true?" This is a fair approach because we want evidence of the truth (whether it's actually true or not). This is called **CONFIRMATION BIAS**. It's a theory that says we see what we want to see, not what is actually the case. We do this to ensure another human need we have, which is protecting our ego. If I have an interpretation that says, "People will judge me for making a mistake," *or* "There's not enough to go around," then unconsciously, I need to prove to myself that I am correct. As a result, I will live my life finding every reason and example that I am right. Why? Because people want to be right. If we are right, then we can't be wrong, and since being wrong brings so much shame and guilt, we tend to avoid it at all costs. We don't want to be wrong, so we'd rather be right, even about the wrong things. By being right, we not only protect our ego, but we also reinforce our original interpretations and begin creating an imaginary safety and security net for ourselves.

Once we've confirmed our suspicions and acknowledge (even unconsciously) that we're right, then we begin to **INTERNALIZE** our bias. Based on our findings, we make it mean something about us personally. We think, "That bad thing happened to me, so *I must be bad*" or "I failed, so *I must be a* *failure*." We've gone from creating an interpretation about the world and the way it works to confirming a suspicion based on more experiences happening around us, seeing what we want to see. Then we internalize it and make it mean something about ourselves and others, which is where so much of the collateral damage occurs.

Once we've internalized all this, we begin to **CONDITION** ourselves, establishing habits, patterns, and routines to coincide with what we think to be true. Then, with enough habits, patterns, and routines, we create **RESULTS** and a reality that proves all of it to be true. We become our own self-fulfilling prophecy because our results point back to our original thought, and then we ride that train to our grave as a belief.

If we summarized the belief formation, it would look something like this:

Experiences + Interpretation + Confirmation Bias +
Internalization + Conditioning = Results

Here's where this gets even stickier.

Research has also shown that 90 percent of our brain develops between the ages of five and eight. Therefore, the quality of our childhood experiences in the first few years of life—positive or negative—shapes how our brain develops. During these formative years, the parts of the brain that are forming include perception, understanding, expression, memory, and cause and effect, which are ultimately responsible for figuring out why things happen the way they do. What's interesting (actually inconvenient, ridiculous, and horrifying) is that we are living our childhood experiences in the form of beliefs as grown adults: mentally, emotionally, spiritually, relationally, and financially.

Basically, this means that the five-to-eight-year-old you—who had an **experience**, created an **interpretation**, lived to find the proof that it was true (**confirmation bias**), made it mean something about yourself (**internalization**), and then created habits and patterns (**conditioning**), —is driving your life today (**results**), whether you are twenty-eight, forty-two, or seventy-five. That means the results you have today, as well as how you view life, marriage, money, people, career, God, and even yourself, have ultimately been unconsciously decided by a five-year-old.

Absurd. I know.

Here's the good news. Knowledge is power, which means you can *now* do something about it. Instead of sitting at home hitting your head against the wall with the "same old, same old," deeply wanting new results but having no idea how to create them. You now have the infrastructure to do so. Remember, you build your life on beliefs and what that tells me is you don't need to change your life; you need to change what you believe.

Here's the hope in all of this:

Anything you want to change, you can change.

Any result you want to create, you can create.

Any dream you have, it can be yours! But you're going to have to go at a seed level, a belief level to create real, lasting change.

Limiting Beliefs

The greatest barrier to change (of any kind) and you living a better life, chasing every dream and desire of your heart, is the unconscious (and even conscious) *limiting beliefs* you hold to be true. I'll say it again: **The *only* thing standing in your way is *not* you; it's the limiting belief you hold to be true.** Your limiting beliefs are where your dreams die.

There is a ton of talk right now in the personal development world about limiting beliefs. This is nothing new, but I am glad we are finally doing justice in spreading the word about these suckers. A limiting belief, by definition, is just that, a belief that limits us. Sounds simple and even manageable, but unfortunately, that couldn't be further from the truth. Limiting beliefs are legit. They are no joke. Limiting beliefs are those walls that hinder us—only they're hidden. They can feel like the one thousand-pound elephant in the room that most of us try to ignore, but given enough time, we can't ignore them because our whole lives are built around them.

Typically, we are running up against a limiting belief when we feel like we can't break through to the next level, we feel stuck in habits and addictive cycles, we're tired of the same results but feel like we don't know how to get new ones, we're unfulfilled, we can't reach a goal, we struggle in our relationships, or can't seem to get healthy or stay healthy. It's what I call "the thing under the thing." The Bible says, "They don't know, neither do they consider "for he has shut their eyes, that they can't see; and their hearts, that they can't understand" (Isaiah 44:18, World English Bible'). These limiting beliefs are like a veil over our eyes that shape our identity and become the lens we make decisions from. It's Satan's way of distracting us, detouring us, and lying to us because if he can get you feeling stuck, addicted, tired, and unfulfilled, then he can stunt and even stop your progress. But notice I said *feel* stuck and *feel* unclear. We aren't *actually* stuck. We just *feel* stuck. But, it shows how loud our limiting beliefs can be.

As you'll come to learn, the "thing" is never the thing. And as you see now with belief formation, much of what you're experiencing today is not just the experience of today, but the impacts of your beliefs established years ago. Understanding your own limiting beliefs is going to be one of the most transformational pieces of information you can learn because you'll finally have one of the keys that unlocks heaven on earth. Anyone who wants to overcome obstacles (including the hurts and mistakes of the past they've been running from), break the habits and patterns that no longer serve them, and ultimately live their wildest dreams *has* to learn how to identify and confront their limiting belief(s).

Most of the time, I hear people complain, explain, or give account for *every* reason why something isn't working; the first thing I ask myself is:

What limiting belief do they hold to be true? I could care less about the reason, excuse, or obstacle because it is meaningless to me. What holds more meaning and power is not "the thing" (the reason, excuse, or obstacle); it's "the thing under the thing"—the belief behind the reasons, excuses, and obstacles. Because of this, every time I get stuck or hold myself back in any way, I have trained myself to ask: *What belief is holding me back and limiting me from where I want to be?* By doing this, I draw consciousness to my beliefs. I shine a light on the dark spot.

Now, why do I start us off with identifying our negative, limiting beliefs as opposed to something, oh, I dunno, a little more light-hearted? Negative experiences have a greater impact on our brains than positive ones. This is called negativity bias. It causes us to hold onto the things that have pained us more so than the things that have brought us joy. This, in turn, causes us to live on guard because we unconsciously believe if it's happened once, it will happen again, putting us in emotional survival mode (whether justifiable or not). Because of this, we have tendencies to behave as if someone is out to get us because we were hurt in our past and are therefore expecting to be hurt in our future. Because we were disappointed or let down years ago, we don't trust anyone and are automatically justifying reasons for why it will happen again. Because we made so many mistakes in our past, we assume we'll do it again and again. This is why we can't get past the "thing" that's standing in front of us today.

The other reason I suggest starting with identifying your limiting beliefs is that, unfortunately, people are cynical and suspicious. So if you started with this beautiful vision for your life, you'd likely shut down and not believe me because "it's too good to be true." It's just the way it goes. So intentionally, I am first going to spend time showing you the power of your negative beliefs, and then that way, it will be much easier for you to grab onto the power of your positive beliefs.

Here's something important to realize before we begin: a limiting belief will never, ever, ever serve you in where you want to go. *However*, it may have *protected* you for a while, therefore, seeming to have a specific purpose in your life. This is also known as a stronghold. A stronghold is something we feel we need to protect. It's something we believe needs to be defended. In layman's terms, if I have a belief about something and I believe it to be true, I'm going to defend it, whether it's true or not. It's human nature. And being that your limiting belief has posed as a "truth" that feels like it's saved your heart from getting broken again and that it's provided you with an answer to a seemingly unanswerable experience, of course you're more likely to hold onto it and protect it. This is why it can be so powerful because it can become twisted and manipulated, causing you to think that it actually protects you, and anything that we feel protects us we tend to want to defend. But if you want to move past it and want to go to the next level of your life in any area, it can't go with you.

Limiting Belief Exercise

As mentioned, by definition, a limiting belief is simply a belief that limits you. You *want* more money, you *want* more impact, you *want* more love, you *want* a healthier body, you *want* more courage and faith, and you *want* to travel more. The list goes on and on, but it ain't happening. There's what feels to be an invisible barrier that you can almost feel as you begin to move toward those things that you desire, but you're just stuck. You feel blocked from the things that you want. I get it.

If you're not willing to look at these blocks—where they come from, what you're making them mean, and the power they have over your life—then you'll never have the insight to break free from them. And you do want to live free, don't you? The good news is, your beliefs have more to do with your freedom than you may think.

With that being said, we are now going to uncover your greatest limiting belief. The way that we do that is by using the Belief Formation Equation (Experiences + Interpretation + Confirmation Bias + Internalization + Conditioning = Results). We'll start by recalling your earliest experience (memory) that you would label as negative, stressful, or traumatic. We all have them, and the only reason I want you to bring this back into your consciousness is that if we don't heighten our awareness around why we do what we do, we can never be free. It doesn't matter how big or small, how stressful or traumatic the memory is. The experience is the experience, and it took a negative toll on you, and rightfully so. You want this experience to have occurred between the ages of five and eight because, as I've pointed out, early formative years have a profound and lasting influence on our development as people.

At this point in the process, I would like you to recall your *earliest* experience (between the ages of five and eight) that you would call negative, stressful, or traumatic and write it here:

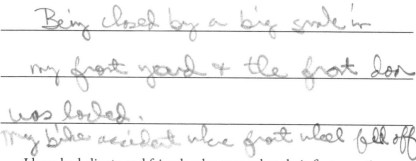

Being closed by a big snake in my front yard + the front door was locked.

My bike accident where front wheel fell off.

    I have had clients and friends who remember their first negative experience being someone making fun of their voice in kindergarten, calling them "squeaky." Another client and friend was sexually abused by an uncle. Another had to consistently take care of his sister because their mom was so emotionally unstable that he was afraid for both their safety. Another speaks of missing the winning goal in a soccer tournament. Another says she remembers having to play the part by going to church as a family every Sunday but feeling like they were hiding the real dysfunction behind their pretty clothes and fake smiles. Another remembers countless moments where her dad, who was overly aggressive, would do everything for her because she was too slow. Each had an experience. It doesn't matter what your experience was; I just want it to be real to you.

After recalling your earliest experience, you are then going to recall or address the *interpretation* you gave to it. Remember, an experience is just an experience until you give it meaning. Once you know the meaning, we will look at all the ways you confirmed it to be true and then solidified patterns, habits, and decisions around that belief. This is all according to the Belief Formation Equation.

I am going to give you my example before you do yours. My earliest **negative experience** was when I was five years old. I can vividly remember playing Barbies with my dad without a care in the world. I don't remember how long we were playing, but at some point, that experience and the joy and carefree attitude I had quickly transitioned as my parents sat me down on the living room couch and told me they were getting a divorce. *That was my experience.*

I can remember sitting there feeling so caught off guard and so mind-boggled. I was only five, mind you, but I remember it like it was yesterday. I felt like a fool. I felt played. I was at a loss for words. It was like I detached from my own body, and every memory from that point on was of me looking in on my own life as if I needed to protect myself. Because I felt I needed to protect myself, I lived from this emotionally made-up vantage point, so I felt like I was always looking in on or down on my life. All I could think at that moment was, *"Life will catch you off guard and completely sideswipe you. Better buckle up and drive, be in control, or be eaten alive."* That was my **interpretation** of that experience, and soon enough, it became my interpretation of the world and the way that it worked.

I then set out on a journey to do anything and everything I could to build a life within my control. I couldn't afford to be wrong, I couldn't afford to be caught off guard, and therefore I executed from very high levels of stress as a kid and throughout most of my early adulthood. My cortisol levels were sky-high. To make matters worse, I learned early on that if I played the part and did everything right, I would get accepted for it, and likewise, if I missed the mark, I got shamed and reprimanded for it. This was my **confirmation**

bias. Hence I was very guarded, and though everybody knew my name, nobody had access to my heart. I was an A student. I said all the right things, did all the right things, and looked like everything was fine on the surface, but I wasn't fine behind the scenes. I felt imprisoned. I wasn't having fun. I didn't feel free, and because I believed I needed to control my world not to be hurt again, I did. I became a learned controller.

I internalized this experience and just about everything else about myself, which resulted in thoughts that sounded like: "I am wrong. I am bad. I am a fraud. I am worth leaving. I am not important." Therefore, I built my world as such until I couldn't hold on any longer, and I fell off the deep end after I graduated high school. My pain became so unprocessed and my thought processes and beliefs so self-deprecating that I just couldn't do it anymore. I became my own self-fulfilling prophecy of "I am bad. I am wrong. I am a fraud." It didn't matter how many Bible verses I knew, opportunities that came my way, how many people reached out to help, or how many moments to make a change were presented to me. My internal reality had already shaped my external reality, and because my internal limiting belief was so strong and so "true," I finally decided it was easier to be bad (**conditioning**) than to pretend I was not. Hence a few hefty years of wrong choices and a legit broken heart (**results**).

You see, our beliefs about ourselves are so powerful that it doesn't matter how much good stuff is going on around us or how many people tell us how good we are. If we feel wrong, bad, or not good enough, and that negative internal conversation is on repeat for long enough, we can't help but mimic that behavior in a very real way. It's a stronghold in our life. Thankfully, I had the pattern interrupt of a lifetime when my husband (sent from God above) walked into my life and gave me the opportunity to lean in and heal from my own self-deprecating beliefs. He gave me the space to think in a different way and pointed me back to God in ways I didn't know I always needed. Together we walked through our own awakening, just like the one I am teaching you now. Though extremely challenging, it was worth every dang minute. I got my life back, and so can you.

Now, it's your turn.

I want you to go back to your earliest experience and consider the interpretation you gave it. In my example story, my experience was "my parents got divorced." My interpretation of that experience was "Life will catch you off guard and sideswipe you, so you better be in control." Your interpretation is the *meaning* behind your own experience. It could be "I am not safe" or "The world is a mean place to those who can't handle themselves" or "Be perfect to be loved." Look back at your negative experience and ask yourself, what did I make that mean? What was my **interpretation**? Write your thoughts here:

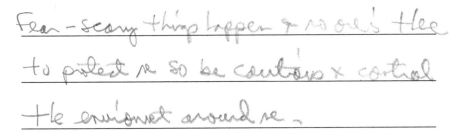

Fear - scary things happen & no one's there
to protect me so be cautious & control
the environment around me.

Now, look at your life over the past twenty to thirty years per that experience and consider any other experiences that proved that interpretation to be "true." This is every boyfriend or girlfriend that broke your heart, every second-place trophy, every letdown, failure, repetitive mistake, every time you didn't chase your dream, habits that didn't serve you, etc. These are the follow-up experiences that seem to confirm your first initial interpretation to be true. This is **confirmation bias**. Write all of those memories here:

2 Divorces - 1 left me, other abused me.

Now, I want you to take some ownership and identify what you made all of this mean about *you* over the years. We do form our own opinion of ourselves, and quite honestly, it's the most powerful opinion we could have. Sure, it sucks when other people don't like us or think we're not worthy or important but what's even worse is when we feel that way toward ourselves. For me, this sounded like "I am not as good as you think I am and when you find out, you're going to leave me." So, per your initial experience, interpretation, and all the confirmation that has happened between then and now, what did you make it mean about *you*? What do *you* say about you? How did you **internalize** this? This will be a statement using "I." Write that here:

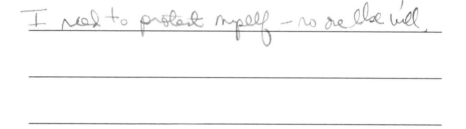

I need to protect myself — no one else will.

There you have it. This is your limiting belief, my friend. This is what keeps you from moving forward. It isn't actually your past. It isn't the person that hurt you. It isn't the economy or your boss. *This belief* is what keeps you from believing the promises of God, making more money, feeling more joy, having a career you can be proud of, experiencing more passion in your marriage, or taking more risks. It's *not* you. It's your own limiting beliefs about you. You are not your own block; it's just the belief about yourself that is blocking you. It's just the thought you've accepted to be true.

It's heartbreaking, I know. The first time I did this, and I recognized how much I had grown to hate myself because "I am not as good as you think I am and when you find out, you're going to leave me" had played in my head for so long, it broke my heart. I was able to see how so much of my life had been lived through this limiting belief. It became clear as day that Satan had used this limiting belief to rob, steal, and destroy from me in so many ways only I hadn't recognized it because it came in the sound of my very own voice. It just crushed me.

You probably feel the same way, and as much as I hate the pain for you, you have to feel the pain and acknowledge it to begin moving forward. The more you ignore it, and the longer you avoid it, the worse it gets. But the sooner you know what you're dealing with and can deal with it head-on, the better off you will be.

Now What?!

If you're like me, or anyone else who has been through this dream work, you're thinking, "What do I do now? Where do I go from here? This changes my perspective on a lot of things. I even see why I do what I do, but now what?" Super fair. This is the consciously incompetent phase we talked about in Chapter 5, remember? Refer back to the tool we call acclimation, and first, allow yourself permission to catch up with this new revelation. Identifying your limiting belief is deep work. It will move you to your core. You are at Base Camp 1, my friend, which means you need to acclimate and let yourself catch up to a new condition, to a new awareness. Make sure you do the work in the workbook as it's designed to help you process this belief and ultimately let it go.

Now, before we move onto establishing a better belief, one that moves you forward, I want you to do a few things to cement this:

First, I want you to reflect on the impact that this limiting belief has had on your life (and currently is having). Why the heck would I want you to do that? Because I have learned that if we don't hate it, we'll tolerate it. If you don't begin to hate this belief, you will continue to tolerate it in your life as you have thus far. So, by taking inventory of its effects, you're much more likely to let it go. On the next page, you'll see The Ripple Effect. You'll see in the smallest of circles there is extra space. I want you to write your limiting belief there. Then I want you to "circle out" and identify in each section how that belief is impacting your family, health, career, etc. Consider the impact it's having in each area of your life, really seeing it for what it is. Then do it again and again.

RIPPLE EFFECT

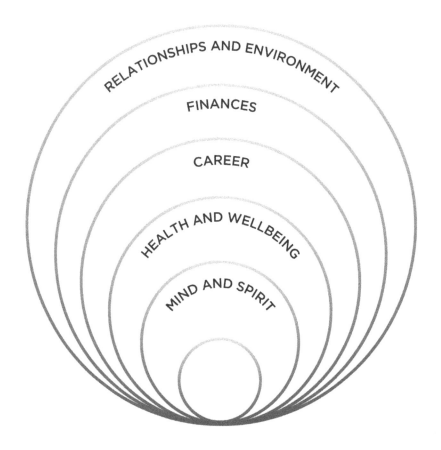

Now that you see the impact of this belief, how do you overcome it? How do you live beyond its ripple effects? Do you want the simple answer? Or as I call it, "the simple, yet stupid, hard answer?" Repentance. You ask God for forgiveness, you forgive yourself, and yes, you even forgive others.

Some call this a spiritual matter, and yes, that would be true, but it's also just a good, sound, humane thing to do. Many voices in the personal and professional development world talk about taking responsibility and owning your mistakes. In theory, this suggestion is a form of repentance but what most fail to do is actually say, "I'm sorry," mean it, *and* change their ways. In order to overcome something, you have to first start with a pure heart of repentance. Repentance looks at the error and wrongdoing, and in this case, the wrong thinking, takes ownership, surrenders at a heart level, says, "I'm sorry," and changes direction. Saying "I'm sorry" in our house means change. It's one thing to say, "I'm sorry," it's another to live like it. It's a repositioning, with resolve, to go in a different direction, which also means that it's the impetous for change. Once you can recognize that you hold your own key to change by simply repenting, it liberates you to live free. So yes, it is a "spiritual matter," but it's also your path to freedom.

Repentance has to start first with you and God. Ask Him to forgive you for your wayward thinking. Ask Him to forgive you for your past choices because of this wayward thinking. Ask Him to forgive you of *all* the things. Asking for forgiveness doesn't make you wrong or bad as a person; it just makes you human. A human who needs a God that forgives seventy times seven times and then some. "If we confess our sins, he is faithful and just and will forgive us our sins and purify us from all unrighteousness" (1 John 1:9). That means, it doesn't matter how much you've done wrong, He is still faithful to forgive you and not because you earned your forgiveness or are more deserving but simply because God sent His son to die for you to cover your sins as a sacrifice. Your repentance just positions you to receive the gift of grace!

In doing this, you begin to see the love of God and the heart He has as a Father, something most of us really don't understand. Why? Because it blows our mind! His love is beyond our cognitive understanding. Though we'll even try to mirror such a love, we will fail because our love is still imperfect. His is not. It is unequivocally perfect in every way. The Bible says, "Though the mountain be shaken and the hills be removed, yet my unfailing love for you will not be shaken" (Isaiah 54:10).

But because most of us have been so busy living from our limiting belief, blaming, shaming, and guilting ourselves for our past mistakes and failures, we can't even fathom such a love so we've just avoided it. But if we, you and me, simply confess our sins, acknowledge the wrong-doing, the wayward thinking, then all we have to do is *accept and receive* forgiveness.

Once you begin to receive His forgiveness, you will begin to see His love. The next step is to begin to forgive yourself so you can love yourself. Most of us have been so busy living from our limiting belief, protecting ourselves, and wronging ourselves for our past mistakes and failures that we unconsciously have developed a subtle hatred for ourselves instead of self-love. In the book of Mark, a teacher of the law asks Jesus, "Of all the commandments, which is the most important?" Jesus replies, "The most important one ... Love the Lord your God with all your heart and with all your soul and with all your mind and with all your strength" (Mark 12:28–30). He then says, and this is what I want you to grab onto, "The second is this: 'Love your neighbor as *yourself.*' There is no commandment greater than these" (Mark 12:31). My question to you is this, how much more can we love those around us if we aren't willing or able to love ourselves first? In order to love yourself, you have to forgive yourself. You have to forgive yourself for your limited thinking. You have to forgive yourself for past behaviors and actions based upon that limited thinking. Obviously, this will be an ongoing process but ultimately, one of the best relationship-building practices you can do for yourself.

Once you can accept His forgiveness freely and begin the process of forgiving yourself, you are liberated to forgive those who have hurt and wronged you. The Bible is very clear about its message in this as it says, "Be kind and compassionate to one another, forgiving each other, just as in Christ God forgave you" (Ephesians 4:32). As we, too, have been forgiven, so we must forgive. For those of you who faced the hard realities that your first experience was out of your control and involved the very people who should've showed you love and care but ultimately stole your trust and innocence, your next step becomes one of love and forgiveness for others. Though

I will encourage you to forgive with your whole heart, this does not justify what someone did or didn't do. It does not make their behavior right. You see, forgiveness doesn't let someone else off the hook; it lets you off the hook. This is why the Bible talks about forgiveness 121 times, *not* because it lets someone else off the hook but because it lets you off the hook. When you learn to forgive, you live free. So if you can trust your process and recognize that your ability to forgive has less to do with them and more to do with you, your life will open back up to you. If you can join me in agreeing that this limiting belief doesn't serve you or make you better, then we can begin the process of letting this belief go by first repenting and then establishing a better belief in its place (which thank God we'll do in the next chapter).

The last thing I want you to do before heading into the next section is to write a letter to that younger version of you who lived your experience. I want you to grab your DREAM: Workbook or Journal, and with that "little you" in mind, I want you to write a letter that does two things:

1. Acknowledge the pain. This means you acknowledge all the pain, all the hurt, and all the disappointment that this "little you" must have (and has) experienced. Bring it all to light. Don't leave anything out. Through my own personal development work, I've learned that the person who needs to acknowledge your needs, pain, and even dreams most is not someone else; it's you. Believe it or not, *nobody* else will ever be able to fully justify or give account for the experiences you've had in this life. Nobody will ever be able to ask for enough forgiveness to make something "wrong" all of a sudden "right." Nobody will be able to provide enough clarity around our deepest questions or give you enough permission to really live your life other than yourself. We are the *only* ones who continue to hold ourselves captive, so the minute we release it is the minute we are free. I want you to write this letter to release all that energy and give yourself, maybe for the first time, the care and attention you needed after a difficult experience. Include in this letter your areas of repentance, for yourself, for others, and from God.

2. Give a new perspective. Once you've said everything you needed to say, I want you to close your letter by giving this "little you" words of hope, love, and a different way of looking at the experience. A perspective that "little you" would, in theory, cling to and would never let go of, thus impacting the way that you would've approached life. We know we can't change what's happened in our past but maybe, just maybe, had you had this perspective of a different truth, you might have navigated the waters of your life differently. Often, more than a change in circumstances, we need a change in our truth. What would you have said to yourself? What did "little you" need to hear in that moment? What would have provided emotional, spiritual, and mental support to you in that moment? If you, right now, could graciously and peacefully come behind "little you" in that moment, whispering a statement of hope and truth, what would you have said to yourself? What would God's truth have said?

Here's an example of my own letter:

Dear Julia,

I am so sorry. I am so sorry you were so caught off guard. It shouldn't have been that way. You were a small child, deserving of nothing more than the space and environment to create and play freely. Your parent's divorce was too heavy of a burden and responsibility for you to take on, and though I see why you did, I am so very sorry that you felt like you had to. I am sorry you felt like you lost your childhood in one fell swoop, and I am so sorry you never felt safe. You had the right to protect yourself. You had the right to control everything. Your parents didn't mean to hurt you. They truly were doing the best they knew how. I am sorry you felt like you had to be perfect. I am sorry that your stress levels were so high that you never got to feel the free beauty that life had to offer you—joy, love, peace, patience, creativity, and faith. I am so sorry that you didn't see yourself as enough or beautiful or even worthy of love. I am so sorry.

Here's what I wish for you. I hope you keep creating. I hope you keep playing. I hope you keep dreaming. I hope you feel safe from the inside out. I hope you don't apologize for being who you are. I hope you can find it in you to trust yourself and to trust God because even in that devastating moment, God was there with His arms of protection and unconditional love wrapped around you, guarding you and keeping you. I hope you can look at life through the windows of safety, to see that you have options, choice, chance, and beauty all around you. I hope you can dream big while also stopping to smell the roses. I hope you know that this is just the beginning. Stay playful. Be powerful. Be bold. Live uninhibitedly and love deeply. Even though you will lose and fail and people, stuff, and experiences will come and go, love will always be the best thing you can keep giving to yourself and to this world, ferociously and unconditionally. Go all in, often. Try and try again. It doesn't need to be perfect. What you want, wants you. God and all of heaven have your back. Get it, girl!!!! LIVE.

Sincerely, the older version, JG

Your turn to write your letter.

From the bottom of my heart, I commend you for gaining awareness that most people don't have the courage to gain. The pros (and cons) of this level of awareness are now you have no one and nothing else to blame (including yourself). The only thing to point blame toward is the belief and *that*, thank God, is changeable. When we point fingers at other people or need justifiable answers, we lose more control and waste more energy because those are things we just cannot change. When we point the blame and judgment finger at ourselves, we imprison ourselves. We don't position ourselves for change or growth because we only feel shame and guilt, and that never propels progress. But by acknowledging our limiting belief(s), what you just did is take the heat off of anyone and anything you cannot control (or change), and you put the attention exactly on the thing that you do have control over—your very own beliefs.

the only
thing standing
in your way
is not you, it's
the limiting belief
you hold to
be true.

CHAPTER 8

Diving into Your Beliefs
Part 2

Understanding and Creating
a Limitless Vision

IF YOU'RE LIKE MOST PEOPLE, turning that page from the last chapter to this one was weighty. Fully understanding a limiting belief can be a lot to digest and a lot to look at, but kudos to you, you did it! Even though there is so much power in our limiting beliefs, acknowledging and fully understanding them starts the process of dismantling them. It's the things we *think* we know that we actually don't fully understand that have the most power over us, which means now that you are finally clear about what has been limiting you, you can actually *do* something about it. You are no longer ignorant or victim to the invisible. It is clear as day.

But now what? We don't want our limiting beliefs leading our lives anymore, but where does one begin? How do you overcome this belief when it feels so real? How do you start making decisions that reflect something different when all you feel familiar with are decisions that reflect the "truth" of this limiting belief? How do you become stronger, bigger, and more capable than this limiting belief that has been unconsciously yet proactively leading your life for years? Remember, as humans, if not careful, we'd prefer a familiar hell to an unfamiliar heaven, so how do we begin to move away from this familiar hell and toward an unfamiliar heaven?

The first step, as mentioned, is repentance. Once I repent of my wrong choices and thought process, I position myself to hear the truth. I turn myself from what was to what could be. I begin the journey of aligning my beliefs with heaven. As I do, we'll pick our tool from Chapter 3, juxtaposition. We'll use it here by turning the coin to see that it really does have two sides: for every *limiting* belief, we have what?

A *limitless* belief, and like a juxtaposition, it has very contrasting effects. Let's take a look.

Limitless means just as it implies, *no* limit. None. No constraints, no boundary lines, no box, no end. Doesn't that sound nice?! Amazing even? I mean, consider for a moment what your life, family, career, and community could look like through the lens of no limit. It opens up a whole new world, doesn't it? It sounds like heaven on earth. So, if it sounds so amazing, why do so few of us reap the benefit of such a life? Honestly, nobody graduates from college with their whole life ahead of them and says, "I think I'll build a life that is mediocre or subpar at best." No one wants to wake up on a Monday, only to wish it was Friday. No one intends to build a life that leaves them feeling unfulfilled. If we're honest, we all want to experience heaven on earth. Why then don't we pursue it with everything on the inside of us? Why do we not shake off the limits, excuses, reasons, and the grip of our past so we can run freely toward something better?

First, it's because of our unconscious limiting beliefs. But now that you've acknowledged yours and it's no longer unconscious, the next step is replacing it.

Statistics have proven that the reason an addict of any kind goes back to their addiction of choice is not that they actually want to but first, because it's familiar (a familiar hell). Second, because they don't replace the void with something else, so the chasm, the space that those choices leave behind, feels extreme and similar to a gaping hole. For example, if someone spent most of their time drinking or doing drugs, when they stop, what do they do with their time? If someone considered to be a workaholic stops working, what do they do with their new-found time? If someone has lived much of their life in anger, worry, doubt, or control, when they begin to let that go, what do you think happens? Many revert to their old ways not because they want to but because they don't intentionally replace it. They don't fill the gap; they don't fill their time with that something fulfilling and progressive.

The same is true for you. Once you identify how much space your limiting belief has taken in all areas of your life, you must concentrate not just on removing it from your life but also on filling yourself back up with something else. By just taking away your limiting belief, even though limiting in nature, it will leave you feeling a bit of a void at first. And nobody wants to feel a void. Therefore, the objective is not to just get rid of your limiting belief, which leaves a gaping hole, but also to replace it with something that feeds your heart and soul. Matthew 12 gives a rather descriptive account for this, "When a defiling evil spirit [your limiting belief], is expelled from someone [when you let it go], it drifts along through the desert looking for an oasis, some unsuspecting soul it can bedevil. When it doesn't find anyone, it says, 'I'll go back to my old haunt.' On return it finds the person spotlessly clean, but vacant. It then runs out and rounds up seven other spirits more evil than itself and they all move in, whooping it up. That person ends up far worse off than if he'd never gotten cleaned up in the first place" (Matthew 12:43–45, MSG [Additions mine]).

This is not just about removing the limiting belief or getting you spotlessly clean. It's about restoring your home with limitless potential, with God in you, heaven on your earth, which means you have to flip the coin.

It'll come down to a very simple yet distinct decision: *Will I choose to live my life limited or limitless?*

If you're like me at all, you choose limitless all day long.

The Bible says, "Therefore, since we are surrounded by such a great cloud of witnesses, let us throw off everything that hinders and the sin that so easily entangles. And let us run with perseverance the race marked out for us, fixing our eyes on Jesus, the pioneer and perfecter of faith" (Hebrews 12:1–2). That is rather clear in its instructions. We are to throw off every limiting belief that entangles us, AND we are to point our attention where it needs to be—on Jesus. Period.

If you agree, then right here, right now, in this chapter, we are going to do just that. We are going to cast our limiting beliefs to the side, and we are going to fill you back up by replacing your limited belief with something much more limitless! We are going to take the hole that your limiting belief has left behind, and we are going to fill it with truth. We are going to take the time, and I am going to provide the space and the insight into helping you understand how to shift your limiting belief into what we'll call your limitless vision.

What is vision and why is it so important?

"Where there is no vision, the people perish" (Proverbs 29:18, KJV).

Since people without vision perish, we better do our due diligence to understand what vision is so we can throw our whole selves at it. A generally accepted definition of the word vision is *to see* and yes that's true but vision goes beyond seeing with your eyes. What most overlook is that it's also the ability to see and even plan with *wisdom* and *imagination*.

There is so much juiciness in that definition! Now, I know I'm a word junkie but come on, that is amazing! When unpacking this definition even more, we'll look at the words within the words and explore the meaning behind imagination and wisdom.

When we imagine something it's actually the act of creating new ideas or concepts that are not physical to our senses. It's the creativity from within. Here's what God's Word says about wisdom, "For the Lord gives wisdom; from his mouth comes knowledge and understanding. He holds success in store for the upright, he is a shield to those whose walk is blameless, for he guards the course of the just and protects the way of his faithful ones. Then you will understand what is right and just and fair—every good path. **For wisdom will enter your heart**, and knowledge will be pleasant to your soul. Discretion will protect you, and understanding will guard you" (Proverbs 2:6–11 [emphasis mine]). When we use imagination coupled with wisdom we actually tie in a groundedness that allows us to make decisions based upon our experiences in *sound* judgment. It gives us the capacity to take our experiences and to filter them in an unbiased, non–attached way.

How many of you would like to think about your future or, heck, even next week, from a place of true imagination and wisdom? How many of you would like to form new ideas and concepts without being dependent on anything you see today but rather being completely creative and resourceful? How many of you would love to make decisions today without any judgment of the past, fear of the future, or useless opinions or biases? How many of you would appreciate heavenly knowledge and understanding?

Suppose we blended all of that together and landed on a definition for limitless vision, taking into consideration all the definitions of the words at play. In that case, limitless vision could be defined as an unbiased, self-transcended, non-attached way to live that allows you to form new ideas, images, and concepts beyond current, external senses and establish a more creative and resourceful approach to life. Another way to say this is vision is heaven on earth.

BOOM.

. . . .

Limitless Vision =
*a. An unbiased, non-attached way to live that allows
you to form new ideas and concepts beyond current,
external senses and establish a more
creative and resourceful approach to life.
b. Heaven on earth.*

. . . .

With this kind of vision, your future is filled with limitless potential. It's brimming with hope! I know that it *feels* like life has handed you a difficult deck of cards, reality looks bleak, sickness and illness have you down and out, you've been hurt in the past, you just lost your job, or you hate your current job, divorce has side-swiped you, disbelief and fear have got you frozen in your daily decision making, and the economy has blown up your plans. Yeah, I get it, but your vision for the future does not care. It can't. None of those things have any bearing on your future. Hopefully, given enough time, and with the support of this chapter, you will develop the same mindset.

Now, when we begin to move in this direction for most people, their skeptic pops up. They begin to see this as "woo woo" or "too emotional" because their basis of understanding starts to become a bit skewed. Let me remind you of a few things. Do you remember how powerful your limiting belief was and still is (if you're not careful)? Do you see how much damage one statement can create in your mind, body, and the life you live? Why do those beliefs seem more valid than a *limitless* vision? Why is it that we look at limitless, positive, forward-moving beliefs as less legitimate when the foundations of both are just the same, equally as powerful, equally as legit, and completely equal in the amount of potential output?

Our limiting beliefs only seem more legitimate because we've practiced them longer, and because we've practiced them longer, they tend to be stronger, making them louder in our life. Because you've been living so much more from your place of limiting beliefs, your limited results are equally as dominant, so it *seems* like it is more powerful. But the reality is, it's only powerful because you've put more attention there, longer. That's it. Take note of that. The bottom line is the power of a belief comes from the ammunition and focus we put behind it, not because it's right or wrong. **What gets your attention gets your life.** So what gets your attention? Whatever is the loudest! If your limiting beliefs are louder than that of your limitless vision, of course they are going to get your attention. But if your limitless vision becomes louder than your limiting beliefs, then it will begin to get your attention. That means, the bigger the vision, the smaller the limiting belief. My aim is to help you shift your focus and attention to a belief that will actually serve you. My aim is to help you identify a limitless vision so you can begin to pull heaven to earth. Then, it will become your job to make that vision so freaking loud that it not only gets your attention but ultimately shapes your life.

Here's why you're going to want vision to completely captivate your attention:

Limitless vision will never hold you captive to your past but rather, it allows you to be a creator of your future because it enables you to ponder a future from a place of imagination and wisdom, from a heavenly perspective. It opens you up to new ideas, images, concepts, choices, and fresh perspectives that enable you to live free because guess what? In Heaven, we're all free.

It is your unapologetic permission to finally live your life, without stipulation or restraint from the things that hold you back (including environment, thought patterns, addictions, and habits). It is your turn-around strategy. Too often, we spend so much of our life running away from things (our past, limiting beliefs, mistakes, guilt, the enemy, etc.), and this vision will now give you something to run toward. Let's face it, running away is exhausting; it's hard, and though it may work for a while by helping you see all the things you *don't* want, it will never support you in running toward the things you *do* want because your focus is still on the wrong things. The minute you turn around and begin running toward something you do want, you realize, holy crap, this is much easier and gets me to where I want to be much faster. It's like the new alarm clock that wakes you up in the morning. It's called your "why," your fire, your reason for getting out of bed.

It sharpens your decision-making. Now that you know where you want to be, you can make decisions from where you're going, not where you've been. It becomes like your new boss and creates clarity on how to make every decision in your life. It becomes your true north.

It is your greater hope in the midst of circumstances. Look up, and you will always find it. It is your joy in the pain, your courage in the midst of the fear, and your "yes," even when everyone else is saying "no." It says in Romans, "For in this hope we were saved. But hope that is seen is no hope at all. Who hopes for what they already have? But if we hope for what we do not yet have, we wait for it patiently. In the same way, the Spirit helps us in our weakness" (Romans 8:24–26). We cannot control what's going on around us. God never promises that, but we can rest assured in the hope that we have and His strength in the midst of our weakness. That means you're now playing a different game than everyone else. Life's circumstances no longer control you because now, it's an inside-out game, which means you find gratitude for every situation because it's there for a reason and has the potential to make you better. Instead of praying for the rain to stop or problems to go away, you decide to play in the rain and consciously choose to engage with the problems, allowing them to make you wiser and stronger because you have a greater vision pulling you forward. You begin to realize that everything, *everything,* starts from within. You no longer need external alignment because you've already got internal alignment. You don't need other people's approval. Why? Because everything you need is already on the inside of you! You have vision.

And the best part of all, your limitless vision becomes the very seed to every single dream you could ever have or will ever have. And because your vision is connected to Heaven, so too are your dreams. This creates sheer alignment.

It's pretty much the best thing since sliced bread.

That's the power of a limitless life. That is the power of a limitless vision. Need I say more? Probably, so I will.

Most of the manifested limitless visions we see today are a byproduct of just that, someone not needing the world to give them the results they wanted most but rather a limitless vision to guide them in creating it. Look at Jesus's vision: "I came so they can have real and eternal life, more and better life than they ever dreamed of" (John 10:10, MSG). That's why He died on the cross, took our shame, our sin, and our shortcomings. He did this so His vision could be manifested, so we could know Him, accept His truth, and live real, more than, better than (abundantly), forever, with Him. The way He lived and died was in direct alignment with His vision.

Look at an example of this in modern society, Amazon's company vision of "Sell everything to everyone." Yep. Pretty sure they accomplished that one. Despite the fact that Amazon only sold books during their first three years in business, they didn't let that stop them from ultimately selling everything to everyone. Why? They had a clear vision that gave them a clear path with which to make decisions. And now we know them today as what? A company that sells everything to everyone!

Muhammad Ali is known for being "the greatest." He was not the greatest when he started, but his vision of being the greatest gave him a lot of clarity for how to live, act, and train, didn't it?! That vision told him who he was before he was the greatest, and it gave him an upper hand because it meant he couldn't let himself settle for anything but that.

Your limitless vision is your way out of any limiting factors that you may have established unconsciously in your life. It is your key and your path to freedom, and just like Amazon or Muhammad Ali, who perhaps both sounded crazy when they got started, proved firsthand how *not* crazy a clear enough vision really can be.

Jesus had many opportunities to tap out. The enemy tempted him constantly. In Luke, Jesus says, "Father, if you are willing, take this cup from me; yet not my will, but yours be done" (Luke 22:42). Just like Jesus, our limitless vision doesn't make everything easier or perfect, but what it does do is absolutely change you from the inside out so *you* are equipped to handle whatever may come at you because it gives you a true north to focus on, instead of that old limiting belief. Jesus's journey was hard. Amazon hasn't had all good days, and Muhammad Ali didn't only have wins in the ring, but their vision for their future was stronger and clearer than any obstacle or limiting belief that got in their way.

It's no secret; life isn't easy, and it doesn't always make sense, but ultimately, the people with the greatest vision thrive because they have an innate ability to see something that others can't, and they have greater purpose because they believe they've got a job to do. We all need something bigger and better driving us on hard days and even, if you're like me, on the mundane days. Vision is a bigger, broader perspective that doesn't just have to do with you, but rather, the greater good of us all.

My question to you is this: Does your vision for your life go that deep? Are you rooted in such unbiased, unapologetic vision that you're oozing it? Is your vision so real to you that you can't *not* create limitless dreams for your life, family, career, and community? Probably not, and that's completely fair because that's why you're reading this book. *If* your answer is no, let me ask you this: Do you *want* your vision to go that deep, or do you just like the idea? Do you *want* to be so rooted in a limitless vision that it trumps any negative, limiting belief? If so, then let's do this!

Identifying Your Limitless Vision

If you remember, limitless vision is heaven on earth. So by having limitless vision, you are actually bringing heaven to this earth.

The Bible says, "Let the little children come to me, and do not hinder them, for the kingdom of God belongs to such as these. Truly I tell you, anyone who will not receive the kingdom of God like a little child will never enter it" (Luke 18:16–17). Why does Jesus say that? What is it about a child that makes the kingdom of God more accessible? I believe it's because children are not predisposed to all the things we are as adults. Children don't have all the judgments, preconceived notions, shame, guilt, fear, worry, and doubt that we do. Children are much more pure. Free. True. So in order to tap into this kind of heavenly perspective for our own limitless vision, we'll go back to the Belief Formation Equation because if it works for our limiting beliefs, guess what? It also works for our limitless beliefs.

As we begin, I want you to recall your earliest **positive experience** (memory), also between the ages of five and eight years old, only this time, I want it to be an experience that you remember being free, pure, and true. This is an experience that was positive, peaceful, and very happy. It doesn't matter how simple or extravagant the experience was. I want you to recall it and to write that experience here:

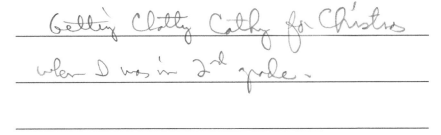

Getting Chatty Cathy for Christmas when I was in 2nd grade.

I have had a few clients who remember their first positive experience being every Sunday at their grandma's house, where they can remember the high levels of love, safety, and security they felt. Another remembers playing a soccer game, shooting the winning goal, and the entire team celebrating their win. Another says he remembers fishing with his dad on a camping trip they did every summer. Another can remember being in school and winning the school spelling bee. As before, each had their own experience, and it doesn't matter what the experience was; I just want it to be real and pure and true.

After recalling your earliest experience, you are going to identify the **interpretation** you gave to it. An experience is just an experience until you give it meaning. Once you know what the meaning is, we will look at all the ways in which you confirmed it to be true and then solidified patterns, habits, and decisions around that belief.

I am going to give you my example before you do yours. Ironically, my earliest **positive experience** was within the same experience as my limiting belief. Only it was that moment I was playing Barbies with my dad (before the bomb of divorce hit). *That was my experience.*

At that moment, I remember feeling completely carefree. I remember having so much fun with my dad. I can remember not having a care in the world and feeling like, "all is well." I felt safe and important. I felt like nothing else mattered other than what we were doing, and we were totally free to be. That was my **interpretation**.

As I reflected upon other experiences that confirmed my interpretation to be true, I could recall family trips to Lake Mohave every year, where we'd boogie board, boat, and play in the water all day long. I could remember the mission trips I went on to the Virgin Islands. I could recall every birthday that my mom went out of her way to make me feel like the most important person in the entire world. I could remember CYT, the Christian Youth Theatre, I was involved in when I lived in San Diego that I just loved. Each memory **confirmed my bias** of my first experience and my interpretation that "all is well" and that "I am safe, I am supported, I am important and free."

Now, it's your turn.

I want you to go back to your earliest experience and consider the interpretation you gave it. In my example story, my experience was "playing Barbies with my dad," and my interpretation of that experience was "All is well, and we are free to be." Your interpretation is the meaning behind the experience. It could be "I feel safe when I am with people I love" or "The world is a beautiful place" or "The magic is when we are together," etc. Look back at your positive experience and then ask yourself, "What

did I make that mean? What was my **interpretation**?" Write your
thoughts here:

First time I remember asking for a gift
+ actually getting it.
I felt heard & loved.

Now, look at your life over the past twenty to thirty years per that experience and consider any other experiences that proved that interpretation
to be "true." This is every family road trip, every first-place trophy, every
joy-filled positive memory you can remember—successes, fun surprises,
every time you chased a dream, hugged a loved one, felt completely seen,
heard, and valued. These are the follow-up experiences that confirmed
your initial interpretation. This is your **confirmation bias**. Write all of
those memories here:

Now, identify what you made all of this mean about *you*. For me, this sounded like "I am safe. I am free to be. I can feel joy and create." So, per your initial experience, interpretation, and all the confirmation that has happened between then and now, what did you make it mean about *you*? What do *you* say about you? How did you **internalize** this? This will be a statement using "I." Write that here:

_____

_____

_____

Some examples would be:

I can live bravely and courageously.

I am enough, as is.

The world is full of limitless possibilities, and I am free to choose.

I am free to do the things that bring me joy.

I live wholeheartedly.

I can go for it because life is too short not to.

This is the start of your limitless vision. Here's how I know. Are the words you just wrote down in contrast to your limiting belief? Do they appear to be the other side of the coin? Do they have the power to light you up? Is it something that you could hang your life on? Does it sound similar to the ending portion of the letter you wrote to "little you?" Does it match what the Word of God says?

If so, then what you have in the palm of your hands is the death of your limiting belief and the birth of your greatest dreams.

Now look at your above words, don't you want that for yourself and also for the world as a whole? Just as your dreams benefit the world around you, so does your limitless vision, and it is designed to explain what the world would look like if you choose to create it unapologetically. One of my favorite definitions of a good vision statement, by Simon Sinek, suggests that it should explain what the whole world would look like if everything we did was wildly successful.

Once you realize that your vision is a seed to manifest anything in this world, you can own the power it has. Look at the above words you wrote and consider a greater impact. It will start to sound something like this:

My limitless vision is to live in a world where we are all free to create uninhibitedly.

My limitless vision is to live in a world where we all do the things that bring us joy.

My limitless vision is to live in a world where we all live wholeheartedly.

Rewrite yours here with the added key words:

_____

_____

_____

As you can see, this has power. Had you had this as a conscious belief when you were five, six, or eight years old, it might have changed a lot. But more importantly, by having this vision now, it changes everything! It now gives you direction and complete resolve about the world you are here to create, and by committing yourself to this vision, not only will you create it, you will demolish your limiting belief.

Now What?

Now that you have your limitless vision, what does that and your dreams have to do with one another? How do they interconnect? As I've mentioned before, your limitless vision is your seed, so by establishing a new worldview, you are creating a much more solid approach to grow your dreams. Your dreams aren't manifesting because you've planted your tree with the seed of your limiting belief. Now, with this limitless vision, you are putting your seed in ground that is fertile, ready, and full of expectation. Get the seed right; get the fruit right. Get a strong limitless vision; get the purest, most real, most wild-at-heart dreams right!

Here's an example of this: one of my greatest dreams has been to write this book. I have been talking about this for years. But dang, I'd be lying if my limiting belief wasn't all over me every time I went to write it. "Who do you think you are? No one is going to listen to you. You're not good enough to write a book." And on and on. It wasn't until after my greatest limitless vision—to live in a world where we are free to be and create uninhibitedly—actually took root that I was able to manifest from that place. Every time I'd pick up my computer to write, I'd hear the faint sound of my limiting belief, but I'd mentally and emotionally grab my limitless vision and remind myself: *I am free. I can create uninhibitedly.* It became my bridge, the connection between heaven and my reality.

The same is true with any dream you begin to chase and manifest. As you begin to do so, you are going to feel flustered, insecure, and triggered to revert to your limiting belief and old mental patterns. Don't let yourself. Instead, use this limitless vision to guide you on your way. "Finally, brothers and sisters, whatever is true, whatever is noble, whatever is right, whatever is pure, whatever is lovely, whatever is admirable—if anything is excellent or praiseworthy—think about such things" (Philippians 4:8).

Now, the choice is up to you, which one will you believe? They both have power. They both will change everything. Which one will you listen to? Which one will have your attention? Which one will you build your life on?

Paying attention to this vision is the first and most important thing you can do. Focus on it as much and as often as you possibly can until you get it to be louder than all other voices. Your thoughts will lead you if you don't lead them. Your limiting belief will create your world unless you empower your limitless vision to do so. This is your one life, my friend. It's deserving of all of your attention! That means you are consciously going to have to work on mastering your mind, our fourth tool until it's in alignment with this vision. Day in and day out, ask yourself, "Is this thought in alignment with my limiting belief or my limitless vision? Is this emotion coming from my limiting belief or my limitless vision?" Pay attention.

Once you do this, you will feel less stimulated to control the things around you. You will feel less triggered by how people interact with you. You will gradually stop seeking for others to affirm you. You will no longer need that apology that you are likely never to get. The external seeking mechanisms will shift because you will start to recognize that everything around you is nothing in comparison to what's going on within you. Your whole life, the way you see it, the way you interact with it, and the way you perceive it is built within the very walls of your mind, and this limitless vision just blew those walls up. And now, my friend, you just set yourself free.

Next, I want you to do two things to cement this new vision for your life. Just as you did with the limiting belief, on the next page, I want you to revisit The Ripple Effect, only this time, I want you to replace your belief with your limitless vision. You'll see in the smallest of circles there is extra space, write your limitless vision and then "circle out," identifying how your limitless vision has the power to impact your family, your health, your career, etc. Consider the potential impact it could have in each area of your life. In doing this exercise, you are likely to get all fired up about it. It should begin to awaken, align, and pull you into a new direction. That's the power of a limitless vision.

RIPPLE EFFECT

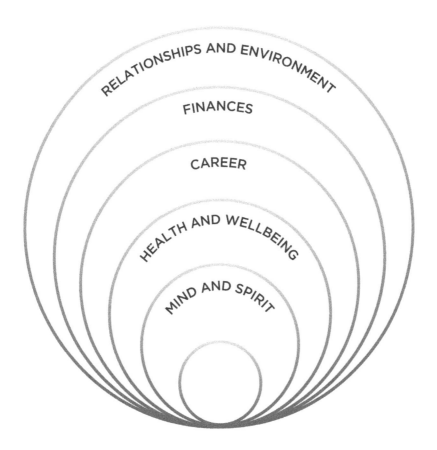

Then, I want you to put your limitless vision everywhere. And I do mean everywhere! The Bible says, "Talk about them when you sit at home and when you walk along the road, when you lie down and when you get up. Tie them as symbols on your hands and bind them on your foreheads. *Write them on the doorframes of your houses and on your gates*" (Deuteronomy 6:7-9 [emphasis mine]). Just as the Bible is emphatic about writing God's commandments on our hearts that we might be mindful of doing everything He asks of us, so too do I want you to be mindful of this vision. Put in on your mirror, hang it on your fridge, put it on your nightstand, carry it in your wallet, and use it as your screensaver. This may sound crazy but give it a color and a smell, find a song that reminds you of it, grab a few Bible verses that embody it. Make it come alive. Put your limitless vision up around your home and office, wear the scent as a reminder, listen to the song morning, noon and night, and recite the Bible verses as often as you can.

Put your limitless vision up around your home and office, wear the scent as a reminder, listen to the song morning, noon and night, and recite the Bible verses as often as you can. Get it loud in your life! Turn the volume up! "Imprint" yourself with your limitless vision as much and as often as you can. Why? We are visual people. We become what we see, and the more you see it, the more it will sink in. The more it sinks in, the more real and natural it will become.

Every morning and night, literally close your eyes and meditate on your limitless vision. Think about it. Feel it. Write about it. Give it your time and energy. When your mind begins to wander, say, "Thank you, but I am choosing to focus on my vision." When circumstances in life try to distract you, someone disappoints you, or circumstances don't go the way you wanted them to go, say, "Thank you, but in the midst of what I see, I choose to believe my limitless vision."

Now, it may not feel normal. It may feel unfamiliar for the first little while. The world around you may not mirror the limitless vision within you. You may notice that your current situation is *not* congruent with your vision. Notice it. Accept it. See the negative ripple effects of it and then take a deep breath because that's normal, but it doesn't have to stay like that. Keep in mind, day after day, you have been executing from your limiting belief, so your results from today didn't just happen overnight. Therefore, just because you start making decisions from your limitless vision today does not mean you will see those effects right away. Sometimes it will take a week, sometimes a month, and sometimes it will take a few years. Be fair with yourself and with this process and let it run its course. The fulfillment of this vision will happen with every aligned decision you make and every dream you clarify, verify, and manifest.

If you're looking for the magic pill and want this to happen overnight, you're setting yourself up for failure in all areas of your life. Your short-sightedness is keeping you from long-term gains. It is easy to forget the power of our daily decisions and the long-term effects of those decisions. For example: if you ate a huge burger today, the effects of that tomorrow would be minimal, especially if you only eat one every once in a while. But if you ate that burger, every day for thirty days, you would absolutely start to see the results of that decision. Or let's say you are not a runner, but you want to run in a marathon. You may only be able to run one mile today, but if you kept at it and ran an extra half mile every day, given enough time, you would cross that finish line. You know that the day you plant a seed and the day you harvest that seed are two completely different days, so do not grow weary in the journey. To grow this seed into fruit will take persistence, pruning, season changes, and a lot of patience.

From experience, the hardest day will be today, the day you begin. The next hardest day is the day you want to quit. Keep at it. Don't quit. Remember the results you were getting from quitting, and remember what you will gain from sticking with it! Remind yourself of who this journey is making you into and what it's going to give you. Then turn off the thoughts in your head that are trying to fool you into quitting, and don't.

Now that we have your seed (limitless vision), let's create some roots, shall we?

the bigger
the
limitless vision,
the
smaller the
limiting belief.

CHAPTER 9

Finding Your Conviction

NOW THAT YOU'VE IDENTIFIED a core limiting belief as well as a limitless vision, it's safe to ask the question, "How do I avoid the limit and run toward the vision? How do I build my life around the limitless vision versus around the belief that is blocking me?" Research has found that we, as people, will do more to avoid loss than to pursue a comparable gain.

The problem with that approach is it will only help us avoid failure, defeat, or keep us alive. It's a very survival-based approach to this life. It's like watching a basketball team play defense the entire game and expecting them to win. Now, I am *no* expert in sports, but I do know this: defense is good, but it will not put a point on the scoreboard.

So how do we put some points up on the scoreboard of life? Now that we have a vision, what do we *do* with it because, as mentioned earlier, "Faith without works *is* dead" (James 2:26, KJV).

The answer is conviction.

I think most would admit they don't necessarily have a problem getting motivated, it's *staying* motivated. Most admit they like the concept of accountability but few actually live accountable lives. How do I know this to be true?

Look at the self-help, motivational industry. Did you know that it is a *$9–$11 billion dollar* industry?? Why? Because people are looking for motivation elsewhere. We're looking for someone else to provide us something we don't think we can provide for ourselves. We're looking for someone to motivate us, hold us accountable, give us the answers, tell us the exact next steps, and feed us the "magic pill" to make everything perfect. Am I suggesting those things are wrong? Well, sort of.

I think it's 1,000,000 percent fair to hire coaches to help us see what we can't see. People who have been there, done that, and can support us in our journey. Heck, I've been labeled a growth coach, so if I didn't totally believe in the legitimacy of it, I wouldn't be one. But, at my core, do I believe that we really need someone else to build our own internal fire or motivation or keep us accountable? No, I don't. We are far greater than the need to spend *$9–$11 billion per year* on that stuff when I know we can find it within ourselves. I'd rather see us spending that money on advancement and growth, innovation, and curiosity.

Let me put it this way, we don't need motivation. We don't even need accountability. What we need is conviction.

I believe we all admire people who live with honest conviction because we have this innate awareness that we should stand for something bigger than ourselves no matter what it might cost us. But how does one go about developing this within themselves? Where do you even start? Well, I think you've got to really understand it in order to develop it.

Conviction means being certain. It's this unshakeable belief that doesn't need evidence because in and of itself, it's completely convinced. Ultimately, this is how you bring an unshakeable, unapologetic, limitless vision to this world, through conviction.

Here is how I define it:

. . . .

Conviction =
a. The ability to stand for something.
b. Your "I can't not."

. . . .

The Bible says, "Therefore put on the full armor of God, so that when the day of evil comes, you may be able to stand your ground, and after you have done everything, to stand. Stand firm then" (Ephesians 6:13-14).

This is how you take your stand. It's what makes you unstoppable in this life. This is your "stick-with-it," your "never gonna give up, won't quit 'til I make it" kind of fire. Conviction is so strong that even the U.S. Supreme Court says our religious convictions are actually protected by the First Amendment of the Constitution but check this out, a preference is not. Why? Because a preference is just an opinion. It's a strong belief but one that will change given enough pressure or stress. A conviction on the other hand will not change, even under the hardest of circumstances, because it's believed to be ordered by God, which is why it's protected by the Constitution. This means that conviction is not just a nice idea, it's a way of life. In other words, conviction is your non-negotiable. It's a duty. It's a call. It's the highest level of accountability because it fuels acts of faith birthed out of such deep-seated belief that what you're doing is ordered by God, heavenly commissioned. Conviction is your "give a damn." It is the ammunition your limitless vision needs. It's something that you *have* to do... Again, it's your *can't not*.

Think of it this way, **if your limitless vision is the seed, your conviction is your root system** grounding everything you believe *as so*. Let's look at the parable of the sower in Matthew. It says, "A farmer went out to sow his seed. As he was scattering the seed, some fell along the path, and the birds came and ate it up. Some fell on the rocky places, where it did not have much soil. It sprang up quickly, because the soil was shallow. But when the sun came up, the plants were scorched, **and they withered because they had no root.**

Other seed fell among thorns, which grew up and choked the young plants. Still other seed fell on good soil, where it produced a crop—a hundred, sixty, or thirty times what was sown… Listen then to what the parable of the sower means: When anyone hears the message about the kingdom and does not understand it, the evil one comes and snatches away what was sown in their heart. This is the seed sown along the path. The seed falling on the rocky ground refers to someone who hears the word and at once receives it with joy. **But since they have no root**, they last only a short time. When trouble or persecution comes because of the word, they quickly fall away. The seed falling among the thorns refers to someone who hears the word, but the worries of this life and the deceitfulness of wealth choke the word, making it unfruitful. But the seed falling on good soil refers to someone who hears the word and understands it. This is the one who produces a crop, yielding a hundred, sixty, or thirty times what was sown" (Matthew 13:3–9, 18–23 [emphasis mine]).

What causes us to "fall away" is not our convictions but rather our preferences, opinions, biases, judgments, and need for instant gratification. We all have dozens of preferences and opinions, some of which are stronger than others but both are susceptible to change with age, peer pressure, experiences, knowledge, etc. Unlike a preference, a conviction won't change.

Our biases and judgments are our viewpoints about something that is not necessarily based on fact or knowledge. It's yours because, well, it's yours. Let's be honest; we all have a lot of biases and judgments but if we're not careful, it's our biases and judgments that begin to build walls. Honest conviction will never build a wall.

Conviction, unlike our desire for instant gratification, is not built in an instant, but rather, over time—something we have a hard time with nowadays. These days we have microwaves, Amazon Prime, DoorDash', and Uber Eats, to name a few. We can have what we want when we want it (even in the middle of the freaking night). Our decisions are more *now*-based than *results*-based. What do I want *now* versus what is the greatest result I want *most*? The problem with this approach is that the path of least resistance will never make us proud. Having what we want when we want it is feeding our ego and our immediate demands but does not give us longevity, persistence, or strength. This is why we lack fire, passion, drive, and hope—which leads to why we're tired, bored, and unmotivated. We're taking the path of least resistance, thinking it will make us proud. Standing in your place of conviction will always make you proud.

So as you can see, our preferences, opinions, biases, judgments, and need for instant gratification are debilitating our strength of conviction, and they're surely not helping us stay motivated or keeping us accountable in any way. Maybe you're reading this now, and you lack motivation, accountability, and drive, or you've got some "juice in the tank" but ultimately fear that you're going lose it or it's going to run out like it always does. Maybe you have even paid for motivation, and it seems to work for a minute, but given enough time, it wears off. Yep. I've been there too. Save yourself a few bucks. **Motivation, inspiration, accountability, and drive don't happen from the outside in. They happen from the inside out.** It's built. It's created. And believe it or not, it *is* sustainable. It's not a fad diet. It's not a burnout approach. It's bigger than that because it starts and stops with you, which means someone or something cannot take it away from you. But that also means it's your responsibility to create and build it.

That means you don't need to be motivated, you don't need an accountability partner, you don't need more opinions, and you don't need to spend more money being inspired by someone else, you need conviction! "Now faith is assurance of things hoped for, a conviction of things not seen" (Hebrews 11:1, American Standard Version).

Building Your Conviction

I know I've already mentioned the movie *Hacksaw Ridge*, but it is a perfect example of how conviction is built. As noted earlier, the movie is a true story based upon a young man, Desmond Doss, who enlists in the army but decides to not bear arms during one of the bloodiest battles of WWII — The Battle of Okinawa. Doss single-handedly saves seventy-five of his own men by evacuating them from the battlefield, without firing or carrying a gun. He believed that while the war was justified, killing was nevertheless wrong. Doss ended up being the first conscientious objector ever to earn the Congressional Medal of Honor.

The part that fascinated me through the whole movie was how unshakable, even unbreakable this young man was. The scene in which he pulls his own men off the battlefield, in the middle of the night, with no one supporting or encouraging him, is extraordinary. But even prior to that, throughout his entire journey, he is hassled, criticized, and even thrown in jail for this decision. When you watch it, knowing it's a true story, it breaks your heart, but he just stands unshakable. Nothing and no one can dissuade him from his decision not to bear arms though they do try. He is beaten, spit on, rejected by his own fellow soldiers, and threatened with imprisonment, but still, he stands by his decision.

How is this level of commitment possible? Most of us quit when it gets even a little uncomfortable, but for Doss, this was beyond uncomfortable, and yet, he didn't give up. Why? How?

He had conviction.

In the last chapter, I said you have been preparing your whole life to live out your wildest dreams? Do you believe that? Do you believe that every setback, challenge, heartbreak, devastation, disappointment, good deed, lesson learned, miracle, opportunity, and chance was divinely pieced together for just the opportune time? Where it eloquently and without human under-standing comes together and works together for your good? Well, I am here to tell you that everything, *everything,* has the power to work together for your good and for the good of those around you. The one prerequisite is to process the pain of the past (which you've already begun by identifying your limiting belief), mix it with hope for the future (limitless vision), and fuel it with conviction, which is built over time and rises to the foreground to be utilized when it's needed most.

Doss didn't just wake up on the day of that battle on Okinawa with some divine inspiration. He didn't roll out of bed that morning, drop his gun and think, "Today is the day that I am never going to carry a gun." He had been preparing his whole life for that moment, trusting that what he believed would carry him on the day he needed it most. The muscle didn't just suddenly show up on that day. He was able to use it on that day because of every opportunity, obstacle, challenge, heartbreak, and insight he had experienced leading up to that day.

In Doss's early years, the movie gives a couple of examples of what I consider "divine moments" that ultimately were opportunities for him to build his conviction. The first is a scene where he and his brother are rough-housing, as most boys do, only for the wrestling to get out of hand, and Doss strikes his brother with a rock, almost killing him. Fast forward a few years, and Doss has an altercation with his dad, a survivor of an earlier war who struggles with alcoholism, PTSD, and depression. As father and son begin to fight, Doss grabs a gun and nearly shoots his dad to protect his own mother. But seconds before he pulls the trigger, he looks up to see one of the Ten Commandments hanging on the wall of his home that reads, "Thou shall not kill." It stops him dead in his tracks. A few scenes later, Doss is presented with an opportunity to rescue a boy from a car, which had fallen on him while he was trying to fix a few parts. Doss courageously runs to the boy's side, creates a tourniquet that stops the blood flow from the boy's leg, and gets him to a hospital.

It's through these *tests of time* that Doss is able to build resiliency in his conviction, so when the war actually happens, and he's literally facing life or death, he stands his ground. And those examples were just the beginning of his testing as his abuse, once he enters the army, only grows worse. The men on his team don't understand Doss's decision or commitment. They see him as a threat and not as a teammate who can protect them in war, but someone who exposes them to weakness and ultimately would do more harm than good. They physically and mentally torture him. They try to break him. But nothing they can do detours Doss from "the thing" he knows he's created to do.

That is conviction.

Once you have your limitless vision locked and loaded, you begin to carry with you a sense of responsibility to make it happen. Vision is great but, in and of itself, is worthless. Yes, vision is insight, it sees something no one else can, but by itself, it can't manifest what it sees without the bearer of that vision taking aligned action and, often, extreme action. Extreme action comes from conviction.

As mentioned, this takes some time, focus, and attention, but once that belief is louder than all other beliefs, you begin to feel as though it is your duty and obligation to bring that world to this world. Your conviction will be your "root system" to do something about it. In referencing our Dream Tree, your vision is like your seed, and your conviction will now be like your root system. A seed with no roots is pointless, but a seed with deep roots can produce an unshakable tree.

If we look at a root system, the roots are designed to absorb nutrients while also anchoring the plant to the ground. The plants that develop a larger root system have greater access to water and nutrients, making them more tolerant of drought or severe storms. Some plants also develop fleshy roots, which can store even more water and nutrients, helping the plant survive tough times. Most plants have a network of thick roots that travel horizontally in every direction. The size and spread of this root system relate to the size of the plant, so generally, the larger the plant, the more extensive the root system.

Conviction, like a root system, is not instant. It takes time to create. It does not come because we are suddenly struck with inspiration, but because pressure, hardship, and different types of stress give it roots so it can bear even greater fruit. Just like our muscles, conviction needs resistance, to the point of failure, to take shape and develop strength.

This is where we will use our second tool—lift 'til failure. The problem for too many of us is that we resist problems instead of seeing the pressure as a privilege. We freak out when we feel pressure. We have sold ourselves a bill of goods that we don't like being uncomfortable and have begun to settle in so many areas of our lives. We hit an obstacle, and it messes with our psyche. We get some resistance, and we freak out. We get a "no," and we make it mean something about our own personal identity. We are rejected, and we carry it with us for years. Others question our ability, and we do the same to ourselves. We play the "busy" card; we avoid, we try to circumvent mistakes and failures. We are only heightening our opinions, preferences, biases, and judgments (fueled by ego and pride) versus building strength in our conviction. Roots need pressure. Muscles need pressure. Your conviction needs pressure. So, my friend, what makes you think you don't need pressure too?

Here is how true conviction is formed:

Founded in experience. Just like our greatest beliefs, our conviction is also built based on the experiences we've had, which is why it will always be in alignment with our greatest vision because it's impacted by the same string of events. Our experiences shape us, both for the good and for the bad; only when we *consciously* live our lives can we begin to use each and every experience to reinforce the conviction we hold to be true.

Developed over time. Just like a muscle, your conviction grows over time and with use. When you believe, "In all things God works for the good of those who love him, who have been called according to his purpose" (Romans 8:28), then you're no longer in resistance but rather trust and acceptance. This allows for every experience to not break you but instead build strength in your conviction. That means every time you encounter opposition, every opportunity that comes your way, the push and pull of the pressures of life, the questions that need answers, the problems that need solutions, all of it is designed to develop the root system of your very soul, producing an insanely strong conviction about the things that matter *most* to you. Once your conviction takes root, you begin to take root. With enough time and focus, water and care, it grows. You grow. It is not instant because it's not supposed to be. We want the roots to take hold. We want to be able to withstand whatever comes our way, and that kind of strength can only be built over time, precept upon precept, step by step. It's in our daily practice, "lifting 'til failure" day after day, that we build our strength.

Strengthened in action. The irony of conviction is that it's only strengthened when you move, take action, or when you do something about it. This tells you that if you feel weak in conviction or limitless vision, thinking about it, even meditating upon it will not strengthen it. Only action will make it stronger. That means you can't sit around waiting to *feel* stronger to *be* stronger; you have to take action, which automatically creates strength, which in turn helps you feel stronger. You will be strengthened in your action.

This proves to us that living in our conviction is the pathway to manifesting our limitless vision. So are you ready not only to clarify your conviction but to strengthen your conviction so your limitless vision can be seen in this world? Let's lean into *your* greatest conviction.

My Conviction Exercise

As we begin, I want you to find a quiet place and excuse your logical brain from this exercise. The logical part of you will not tap into the soulful side of you, so politely uninvite it. Then I want you to recall my statement when

I said that we all admire people with honest conviction…

What about you? Who do you admire most?

I want you to take a handful of minutes to visualize your answer. Don't rush the process. This could be someone you've never met but have only seen on TV, in interviews, or you've read books about them; this could be someone you used to know, want to know more, or is currently active in your life; they could be dead or alive; fiction or non-fiction. It doesn't matter who they are or how much you knew/know them, but you would say you absolutely admire them. Take however much time you need and then write their name down here:

Esther — Gideon

My husband Carl

Next, I want you to write down as much as you can about *why* you admire this person. Write down every last reason you can think of. Why do you admire them? How do they live? How do they think? What are the attributes you admire most? What have they accomplished that you admire most? Write your answers here:

Great! Now, reflect upon all the things you admire about them. Perhaps it's their successes, how they make decisions, the way they live their life, or their life choices. Next, imagine their belief system. What is their greatest belief about life that has helped them have such amazing results? Another way to say that is, what would they say they believed about life that would have supported their approach in getting the results they have? As you well know, we all have beliefs we build our life on. Every once and a while, we find those people who had the courage to live their life from a place of authenticity and alignment, and that's why you admire them. They must have believed something to be, do, live, act, and achieve all they did. What could that be?

To support you in gaining your own clarity, I'll give you my example. The person I admire the most is Martin Luther King Jr. *Everything* about that man inspires me, his tenacity, his grit, his unapologetic fight for justice, and even the fact that his life was messy. He was human. He was not a saint, but he had a dream, and he was committed to that dream. Even though he saw nothing that told him his dream was possible, he pursued it like he was guaranteed a positive outcome. He is who I admire most.

When I considered his belief system or what he might tell me if I asked him *how* he did it, I envisioned him saying to me: "Dig down deep in your heart and pull to the surface whatever it is you find that you care about most, any injustice, mistreatment, unfair advantage, passion you might have, and chase it with everything you've got. And then, don't stop!"

Your turn. Go back to the person you admire most and consider posing these questions to them: *"How did you do it? How have you lived your life in such extraordinary ways? What did you believe to be true about life?"* What would they say? Write the answer you think they would give here (and again, disinvite the logical part of your brain from this exercise):

Now, considering that, and reviewing your answer, if you had to put the above verbiage into a rather concise statement—a conviction statement—with two to five words that intentionally summarized what this person might say, what would it say?

After review of my own answer, here's what I came up with:

Live Free.

Write your answer here:

Live (what)?

Live:

Here's how you know this conviction to be real: Do you remember all those memories I had you recall back in the limiting belief chapter? I had asked you to write down all the experiences that reinforced your limiting belief to be true. If you could go back to those exact moments and now see them not as bad experiences but as moments given to you to strengthen your conviction, does it start to add up? Do the dots of your life begin to connect? They should.

Remember, our conviction is built over time, right in the thick of life, designed not to take us out but to strengthen us and to point us toward the things that are most important to us. Could this conviction statement have been the root system you needed to sustain the obstacles, challenges, and stress you faced?

I also want you to consider all the good experiences you've had thus far in your life. Recall those moments you're most proud of, the ones that are some of your best memories. Were you living from this place? Was your conviction showing up in those times, and now, maybe for the first time, you're able to recognize it?

Live: Bold

Live: Joy

Live: Wholehearted

Live: Valued

Live: Clear

All of these are conviction statements from the people I have had the honor to work alongside. This is the root system for people who are now living unapologetically bold, joyful, wholehearted, valued, and clear because they just *"can't not."* No matter what.

For repetition sake, write your conviction statement again, here:

_____

_____

_____

How do I utilize my conviction in day to day life?

Once a person lands on their conviction statement, the tendencies are to feel good, free, clear. Great. That's what we want. That's what a real conviction statement is designed to do. But if you remember, this is not just about *feeling* good; it's about *being* good. It's not about motivation that will come and go. This is about building a root system that will support you when you need it most, and the way that you build your root system is by using it, by applying pressure. That means, for most of us, we have the opportunity to strengthen our conviction every single day if we're conscious to it. So, upon clarifying your conviction statement, I follow up with one straightforward statement: prove it.

Prove it? Yes, prove it.

You say, "Live: Bold," "Live: Joy," "Live: Wholeheartedly," and to that, I would say, "Great! Now prove it to me!" Prove to me that you mean business. Prove to me in the midst of crisis, change, the unknown, a heated conversation, in times of lack, in moments of stress, even in the good times, prove to me that you believe what you believe. Don't tell me you believe it; show me you believe it. Show me that it is God-ordained. Lift 'til failure baby!

That normally stops a few people in their tracks because it resonates on such a deep level. Do you really believe, above all else, that boldness will help you in hard situations? Do you really believe that joy is the answer even in the hard circumstances of life? To myself, I always say, "JG, do you believe that living free is really the answer?" I phrase it in such a way because I believe it encourages me to dig deeper, to let the strength of the trial build me, not break me. I use whatever is in front of me to verify and clarify that yes, YES, I BELIEVE! This is what causes us to rise up. This is what causes us to stand up in our lives and to be accounted for. This is where conviction is grown! So to you, I would say, "Do you believe it?" If so, prove it! Show me! Do one more push-up!

If you can get yourself to agree that you believe it, even when your head is freaking out, even when your ego wants to run and hide, even when your mind tries to tell you that you're not able or capable, even then, then you will build an unstoppable strength. If you can teach yourself to make decisions from your place of conviction, you can rest assured that automatically you'll be in alignment with your limitless vision. If you're in alignment with your limitless vision, you're automatically standing against your greatest limiting belief, and that, my friend, is exactly where we want you! So when life presents you with "opportunities," when you feel emotions rising, when you feel like you want to run or avoid, when you notice yourself overcompensating or under compensating, when you want to give up, these are all just signals we'll call your "triggers." Like the bumper marks on the side of the road, they are there to warn you of danger. But you must catch the signal, and you must choose your lane! What do you believe?

Remember the parable of the sower quoted earlier, when Jesus said, "But blessed are your eyes because they see, and your ears because they hear. For truly I tell you, many prophets and righteous people longed to see what you see but did not see it, and to hear you hear but did not hear it… When anyone hears the message about the kingdom and does not understand it, the evil one comes and snatches away what was sown in their heart… Since they have no root, they last only a short time." You work your conviction, and guess what, it'll take root and whenever you're presented with the opportunity to strengthen your conviction, you then remind yourself, "I BELIEVE!"

Once you recognize that life's circumstances are all just opportunities presented to you, helping you strengthen your conviction, I want you to do what most people don't do, and I want you to offer up gratitude. This is exactly what James meant when he said, "Consider it pure joy, my brothers and sisters, whenever you face trials of many kinds, because you know that the testing of your faith produces perseverance. Let perseverance finish its work so that you may be mature and complete, not lacking anything" (James 1:2–4).

Note that the verse says, "Consider it pure joy … whenever you face trials of many kinds." That means being grateful in the midst of it all because, "The testing of your faith develops perseverance." Perseverance means persistence in doing something *despite* difficulty or delay in achieving success. Sticking with it, *despite*. This is where your conviction is strengthened.

Whatever is in front of you, whatever obstacle, challenge, opportunity you're facing, with everything in you, you are going to recognize that this isn't happening *to* you; it's happening *for* you. Therefore, you offer up gratitude because it's allowing you to be "mature and complete, not lacking anything." So instead of being mad at the situation or circumstance, God, your parents, boss, cousin's sister's friend, or whoever is (or isn't) involved in what's "happening to you," why don't you instead say: "THANK YOU. This is happening for me, and it's giving me the chance to strengthen myself and strengthen my conviction."

As you consider your own conviction, I want you to tell me five things you will *start* doing to stay 100 percent in alignment with your conviction. How might this change your career or how you spend your time? How would this impact the way you make decisions or respond to people? What habits would you pick up? What would you do even if you were afraid? What food would you eat more of? Less of? How would this shape your goals? List those five (or more) things here:

_____

_____

_____

_____

_____

Next, give me five things you will *stop* doing. Do you remember our analogy of climbing Mt. Everest? If you remember, at each camp, climbers don't add gear; they take it off. Their ascent to the top is about their willingness to let go of the things that no longer serve them so they can sustain the weightiness of the climb itself. What about you? What are you willing to let go of? What things are you holding onto that are not in alignment with your conviction? What judgments are no longer serving you? What opinions serve your ego but don't serve your progress? What biases have you built that don't give you the freedom and flexibility to live your life from conviction? What habits and routines need to go? What thought processes and relationships aren't serving the greater good? List those five (or more) things here:

_____

_____

_____

_____

_____

Now, I want you to really review everything you wrote down, and I want you to honestly ask yourself one powerful question: *Am I INTERESTED, or am I COMMITTED?*

Please note, I did not ask you if you were currently living your conviction. I specifically did not ask you that because I wouldn't expect you to be—*yet*. This is all still new. You've just barely woken up to these levels of consciousness, so this is not about if you are currently living in it or not. I am asking more from a place of, as you move forward, are you in? Knowing what you now know, could you get behind this? Could you hang your life on it?

Second note, I asked you a very intentional question. One that needs further review: Are you *interested*, or are you *committed*?

If you are only *interested* in living from your conviction, you *will* give up. No questions asked, and I'd arm wrestle you to prove it. If you are only interested in something, it does not mean you're actually committed, it just means you're curious about it. How many of you know, if you're only curious about marriage, you probably shouldn't get married? If you're only curious about losing weight, it's probably not sustainable when the presented menu of options hits your table. If you're interested in living out your limitless vision and conviction, the storms of life will present themselves to you, and you'll look for stage left. It will get uncomfortable, your ego won't like it, and you will find a reason, excuse, or justification to find a way out versus through. The hard part about interest is that given enough pressure or discomfort, someone who is only interested will likely give up.

Commitment, on the other hand, means you're in, 100 percent. It's *complete* loyalty. It's *wholehearted* dedication. Note, I said whole*hearted* dedication, not whole *headed*. Commitment doesn't always make logical sense. That's the beauty and the power behind it. True commitment to someone or something is like turning off the mind chatter of the brain, so you no longer have to wrestle with it, rethink it, control it, predict it, or justify it. You just do it, which is why it's so powerful. The moment you *decide* to be committed (because that's all commitment is, a decision), there's no out, no stage left, no tap-out strategies you could create for yourself, no reason, excuse, or justification that is big enough. Sure, you may have to reroute or reconsider your strategy but quitting is not an option. Just like conviction, this level of commitment is an internal issue. Interested is an external issue. It sounds nice, it looks nice, geez, it must be nice, but it's not completely convinced, whereas commitment says, "It IS nice, and I am in 100 percent!"

Think about that business you've always wanted to start, the impact you've always wanted to make, the body you've always dreamed of, the dream home you've always wanted, the career path, or influence you've desired. Think about the family you want to have, the book you want to write, the kind of friend you want to be; all of those things take time, and nothing serves time more than commitment. We need you committed. We need you convicted. If you don't stand for something, you'll fall for anything.

As you set out to grow your roots, growing rooted in your greatest limitless vision, let me remind you of a few guiding principles.

Do not be a jerk with your conviction. True conviction is birthed from *divine* love, grace, peace, and joy because it comes from God, so it's not your hall pass to criticize or manipulate. This means judging other people who don't live according to your conviction is off the table. Your walls won't do you any good. Opinions and preferences? Sure, you can hate sushi, and you can prefer West Coast over East Coast, country music over R&B, skinny jeans over bell-bottoms, but all those opinions that you throw at everybody else, please consider using them in progressive ways or losing them altogether. Your opinions, biases, judgments, and even preferences, if you're not careful, will compartmentalize your life into what you like, what you don't like, who you like, and who you don't like. With every conscious and unconscious opinion, bias, judgment, and preference, you build a wall and suffocate the human spirit, which is comprised of curiosity, freedom, and divine love. No one will remember your opinions, but your conviction has the power to be remembered by everyone. Just like with Martin Luther King Jr., it wasn't his opinions that we all know and remember today; it was his conviction.

Conviction has less to do with convincing other people and more to do with convincing yourself (so lay off everybody else, would you?!). Great leadership isn't about stopping to convince everyone else or pushing your agenda onto someone; it's about being so convicted in action that people can't help but want to follow you. People follow people who are most convicted (not who are most "right" or successful). Conviction is not about agreeing or disagreeing; it's about being true to yourself and what God called you to do and letting that be enough.

Do not hurt, steal, or kill to serve your conviction's purpose. True conviction, used in its purest form, does not need to hurt someone else to be fully manifested and expressed. When done the right way, conviction serves you and the greater good, which means it moves all of humanity forward. (Please note that people running planes into buildings and killing thousands of people may be convicted, but they are not moving humanity forward; therefore, they're out of alignment).

Let your conviction guide you in making better, more aligned decisions out of belief, not emotion. You're allowed to *feel* anger, fear, sadness, bitterness, resentment, or any similar emotions on your journey, but your conviction will be your checks and balances not to make decisions from your emotions. Feel your emotions, yes. Process your emotions, please. But don't let yourself take action from this place or consume more of your energy than necessary. Learn instead to make decisions out of your conviction, not your emotions.

Let your conviction teach you a thing or two about patience. The result of your conviction will take time. It is not an "overnight success," so be prepared to learn patience. Don't rush the process. Learn to trust it, and learn to trust yourself. Most of all, learn to trust God.

Here's to you and living convicted!

Conviction is the
fuel you need to follow
your **DREAMS**.
It's your
stick-with-it, never
gonna give up, won't
quit 'til I make it.

It's your can't not.

CHAPTER 10

Identifying Your Protest

HERE'S THE REALITY OF CONVICTION, as you've just learned: it is a powerful force and does *not* get enough credit. It also does not stand alone. It has a counterpart, a sidekick, a partner in crime, if you will, which means it's only half the equation.

Since you can now recognize that you stand *for* something, wouldn't it also make sense that in standing for something, you are also standing *against* something? We'll put it this way, **in standing *for* something, you automatically stand *against* something.**

Initially, most people struggle with the concept I'm about to teach because they don't like the idea of "standing against something." It feels too confrontational, too abrupt, too forthright, but truth be told, most of us aren't holding the line enough. The Bible says, "Put on the full armor of God, so that you will be able to *stand firm against* the schemes of the devil" (Ephesians 6:11 [emphasis mine]). Believe it or not, we are actually called to live our lives standing against the issues that are not in alignment with our dreams and ultimately, with what God is doing.

It's likely that in *not* standing against something, it can be easy for one of three things to happen:

- You become indifferent about the things that need change in your life, faith, family, career, or community.

- You sit around and complain about all the things you don't like without doing anything about them.

- You overcompensate, doing too much for too many people, resulting in burnouts and less than ideal results.

But if we're honest, we've all got one, or three, or ten areas within our lives where we desire change. For just a second, I want you to honestly consider the areas in your life, faith, family, career, community, and even world where you desire change.

What things don't seem to be working? What issues are being ignored? What strategies are broken? What parts are just unfulfilling? What area in your life needs a change, and it seems as though it won't change? Write your answers here:

_____

_____

_____

Why do we allow those things in our lives to continue? Or maybe a better way to ask that question is, why do *you* allow those things in *your* life to continue?

Do you want to know the honest truth?

It's because you don't hate it enough.

You tolerate it.

By tolerating something we actually allow it in our lives even though we don't like it. Because that sounds like a great life? NOT! Ladies and gentlemen, if we're honest, we are tolerating way too many things in our lives, and as long as we tolerate these things, we won't change any of them. It's actually our indifference that will kill us.

It's been proven that the two greatest motivators in this life are pain and pleasure. That tells us that when we *want* to change but aren't taking the necessary steps *to* change, we either don't hate our current situation enough to change it (pain) *or* the benefit doesn't clearly outweigh the current circumstances (pleasure). This means we literally either have to hate something so much to make a change, or we have to be so elated, so dang excited, that we can't *not* change.

Conviction in that sense is our pleasure play because it's our "I just can't not do it." But what about the reverse? How do we create healthy pain that also supports us in creating change? Is there even such a thing?

Fortunately yes. If you stand for something—conviction—then what you stand against is called a protest—a *wholehearted* protest.

I first dove into this idea over four years ago after I was given a Danielle LaPorte Truthbomb Card Deck. It read, "Passionately Protest Mediocrity." It was as though that card was speaking to my soul. It was as if a light turned on within me, and my hatred was finally set free, for the first time. Note that

I said hatred, not anger, something we are going to talk a lot about in the pages to come.

We all know that a protest happens when a group of people gather together to express disapproval of something. It typically includes a mob of people publicly expressing their objection toward an idea or action and unfortunately, a lot of those protests hit the headlines not because they are handled well but because of the sheer outrage and anger that wreaks havoc on people, neighborhoods, and cities alike. Though they can start out peacefully, many end up being dangerous and highly subjective, often not helpful in either the short or long term. The aftermath seems to create only more issues and hurt more people, and the ripple effects of anger, rage, and destruction only continue. It affirms where someone, or a group of people, stands on an issue, but it doesn't always result in positive, lasting change.

Now, when I'm talking about protesting, I'm not just suggesting a big mob of people walking the streets publicly stating their opinion. In fact, I don't think we need more public protests. I think we need more individualized change at a much more personalized level, so what I'm suggesting is initiating protests in our own lives. And not just any ol' area, but *every* area where you crave change! That's right, my friend, it's time to start a protest, a wholehearted protest, which allows for you to *be* the change, not simply to wish for change.

Starting A Wholehearted Protest

Starting a healthy, wholehearted protest in any area of your life requires four important ingredients: processed pain, wholehearted hate, divine love, and insane clarity of purpose and passion.

What is processed pain?

Believe it or not, some of the greatest dreams that came true in history were actually built during some of the hardest times, during a time of lack, loss, and even suffering. "How?" you ask. How is it possible to build our dreams in the midst of so much pain? Well, it's not built from just straight-up pain but rather *processed pain*, pain that is *willing*. Pain *can* be given purpose *if you heal*. If you look at our previous examples—Desmond Doss, Jason Russell, Martin Luther King Jr.,—these individuals built insane impact specifically from their place of pain, and they did it with love, kindness, passion, and with so much purpose. What does that tell us? It tells us not to avoid our pain but rather to process it and use it for good. That's the way to redeem it.

In my own life, I've learned that my pain, left to itself, does me no good and, in fact, actually causes more harm than good. The same is true for you. Pain left as pain at the doorstep of your life just creates a ripple effect of more pain. "Hurt people hurt people." But when you realize that pain doesn't have to stay the way it is, that you can do something with it, it changes everything.

Here's why pain is such a motivator: when we are hurt or wronged at a deep level, intentionally or unintentionally, it moves us to our core, ultimately shaping who we are. That's why pain changes us. That's why our limiting belief is so powerful because it was built from an experience that hurt us. For most, if we're not careful, we just let our pain sit within us, and we never heal. We never do anything with it, so it festers and grows under the surface, infecting other areas of our lives. It creates anger.

But when you begin to allow the healing process to happen, you find that you're actually able to dream again. Your willingness gives you a fresh perspective. It's in your wholeness that you're able to see many of the answers to the questions you've been seeking and you become unstoppable because now your pain, interlocked with conviction, becomes a place of power.

But, how do you heal?

Though I'm going to give you steps toward your own healing journey, please know that I am not belittling the healing process by dumbing it down to a 1-2-3-step guide, nor am I comparing it to a blue pill or a get rich quick scheme. It's not. The healing process is just that, *a process*. Truth be told, there is no 1-2-3-step guide to healing. It's simply giving yourself the space to do so and learning to trust yourself and God in the process. Too often, we want these 1-2-3-step guides to tell us exactly what to do and when to do it, and we overlook the chance to let God direct our steps. We become so preoccupied with the 1-2-3-steps within the guide, forgetting that *He* is the guide. I encourage you not to take this so literally that you become more dependent on the steps, only to miss out on the healing itself. It's not about the steps; it's about the healing. Also, if you find that you are trying to rush through the healing process, not fully feeling it, not experiencing all of it, or attempting to let it just run its course without actually dealing with it, you are not truly healing.

The first step toward processing your pain and letting the healing happen is to *hear yourself*.

As mentioned, unprocessed pain that merely sits at the doorstep of our lives as hurt and disappointment ultimately turns into anger. Too often, our anger then causes us unconsciously to become externally focused. We begin to focus more on what's going on around us while becoming less focused on what's going on within us. The problem with this approach is we are trying to fix everything around us and doing nothing with the pain going on within us. We shift into avoidance, comparison, doubt, fear, and become really, really busy. But if we want to create a better life and make the necessary changes, we can no longer work from the outside in. We have to work from the inside out. The good news is you're no longer responsible for fixing other people. You don't need to fix the situation. You don't even need to fix yourself. What you need to do is to really, truly hear yourself. That's how you heal. You deal with your pain. You face your hurt, disappointment, and anger for your own healing's sake.

You need to hear your anger. You need to hear your pain. The resentment. The disappointment. The reasons you have felt abandoned, mistreated, over-looked—all of it. Express your areas of confusion, doubt, guilt, fear—all of it.

You need to hear you. You can hang, I promise.

You need to let God hear you. He, too, can hang, I promise.

What are you trying to say?

I have done this process one of three ways, all of which are very applicable for anyone ready to heal and allows you to use the fourth tool in your toolbox of mastering your mind. By hearing yourself, you're actually able to check every thought at the door of your life to see if you really want it to make a home within you. The first way is to grab a pen and journal and write it all out. Let every single word fall on the pages of your journal until there's none left. The second way is to literally walk and talk, with yourself and with God. I know that may sound crazy but believe me, what's crazy is living your life with it all bottled up. Get outside in the woods or a path near your home and just let 'er rain. The Bible says, "The righteous cry out, and the Lord hears them; he delivers them from all their troubles. The Lord is close to the brokenhearted and saves those who are crushed in spirit" (Psalms 34:17-18). Don't just speak the words in your mind; speak them with your mouth, cry out! The third way is to find a trusted someone, maybe your spouse, a counselor, or pastor, and share with them that you need to heal, but you don't need them to answer you or respond. You just need a safe place to hear yourself so you can heal.

Hearing yourself may sound like: "I am so angry! I am so disappointed! I am angry that I have had to live on guard. I am disappointed that I don't feel valuable to my dad. I am upset that I feel like I have to take care of my mom. I am frustrated that I have no money in the bank and tons of potential on the inside of me. I am disappointed in myself for the decisions I've made. I am angry that I don't hear God's voice. I am sad that I keep pushing people away." And on and on.

You'll find in these moments of hearing yourself that it's not about being "right" but rather, being heard. Don't listen to yourself like it's a fact. Don't shame, blame, guilt yourself, and don't judge what comes up and out, just *hear to heal.*

Do you want to shine? Let the hurt within you come out of you so your whole heart can shine within you. Don't push it down or push it away. Don't avoid it or run from it. Hear it. Hear *you.*

The next step is to let the pain teach you and strengthen you.

Once you hear all that you need to hear, you can start building strength by learning the presented lesson. Believe it or not, the healing process *is* teaching you about you, and it *is* building connections within yourself that you didn't even know you needed.

I am a firm believer that if we keep experiencing the same thing over and over again, we aren't learning the lesson. If we aren't learning the lesson, we aren't healing, so when the pain comes up, when you feel the anger or disappointment arise, when current circumstances trigger old memories and emotions, start asking yourself: *What do I still need to learn? What is my pain trying to teach me in order for me to be whole?*

Your pain will always ping you to try to get your attention, and I am encouraging you to use it as a teaching moment because when you become a student of your pain, and you're willing to learn what the pain actually means, you begin to channel it for good. You begin to recognize there is an area within you still left undone, a lie that still needs truth, an area that needs attention, a place within you that desires change. If you no longer blame yourself, someone, or something else but can use it as a lesson (one you need to learn), you actually strengthen yourself.

If you can look at each place of pain as a way to learn something, you no longer *resist* it and instead can *accept* it. It's in your acceptance and willingness that you begin to move the needle of change in any area of hurt. You begin to see the beauty of every lesson, and that allows for the release of the healing process to happen because you'll feel a literal release within you. And it's a good thing because as you go out into this world as a creator and a dreamer, you are going to need to sustain yourself during your creation phase. This creation phase is about building and maintaining what you see within you in the world around you, and if you haven't developed strength in your healing phase, the rest won't last. By learning the lesson, you strengthen yourself. By running from it, you weaken yourself.

Next, use the lesson to get grounded in truth!

Once you're willing and open to learning the lesson, you can get grounded in the truth. You and I both know that your unprocessed pain has kept you in a lie. It's telling you all those limiting beliefs—"I'm not enough. I'm a disappointment. I can't trust other people. Nothing good happens to me." Though these beliefs may seem familiar, they're lies nonetheless. Once you can see these as lies and begin to let them go, you will then have the ability to lean into the truth. The Bible says, "But whose delight is in the law of the Lord, and who meditates on his law day and night. That person is like a tree planted by streams of water, which yields its fruit in season and whose leaf does not wither—whatever they do prospers" (Psalm 1:2-3). Get planted in His truth. Let go of the limiting beliefs and grab your limitless vision. Let go of the lies and grab God's truth. When you finally let go of the things that no longer serve you, you actually have the space and ability to grab onto something new. The whole world will open up to you and the things you once knew as a concept (hope, faith, love) will become real. How will you *know* when you're grounded in the truth? Simple. The Bible says, "If you hold to my teaching ... Then you will know the truth, and the truth will set you free" (John 8:31–32). When you know the truth, you will *feel* free. If you don't feel free, it's not the truth.

Once you know the truth, it's time to give your pain purpose, in word and deed!

Once you know the truth, once you start to feel, see, taste, and touch true revelation, you can't *not* share it. It's like experiencing an amazing restaurant, listening to an incredible song, or reading a great book. What do we do? We share it! Why? Because why would we not share something amazing with those around us? Once you know the truth and it sets you free, you will be compelled to share it with others! It becomes the channel for your own crazy, beautiful, insane purpose! Because you now see more clearly, you'll start to love harder. You'll find new opportunities to serve your gift. You'll share your story, and guess what, you'll give your pain purpose in word *and* deed. This is where true impact and change is created because now, you're not a wrecking ball or time bomb waiting to go off; you're healed. That means you're able to lead with an open heart and an open mind. You're able to take your pain and give it meaning by serving it to the world. And believe me, we need more leaders leading from this place, from a healed place.

And then, you rinse and repeat as many times as you need to.

We are human, which means things are going to come up. We are going to be triggered. New circumstances can easily bring us back to old habits, patterns, and old ways of doing things, which is why the Bible tells us to, "Set your minds on things above." (Colossians 3:2) I mean, for real, it says, "set." That is a seriously proactive word with clear instructions. You can just see heaven saying, "Hey! Put your mind on us, up here! Not over there. Not on things down around you. Up here! This is where the action is." When should we do this? Daily. Why? Because we're human, and we need a clean mind every day. Just like you take a shower and brush your teeth every day, your mind and heart also need to be cleaned every day. Do not let your ego get in the way or make you believe that you should be stronger, that you should have it all together. Don't worry about being stronger at the expense of not being a real human being. I'd rather you be real than strong. And the irony is, the more real you become, the stronger you will be! When things come up, go back to Step 1. When people offend you, circumstances trigger you, or when anger arises, rinse and repeat this whole process as soon as you can see it happening. This will keep you healed!

Your pain is never wasted unless you choose to waste it. Your pain has the power to shift your life, your family, your career, your community, and even the world. My question is, will you use it for good, or will you just let it fester and infect your life? Once you begin your healing journey and commit to sticking with it for as long as you're on this planet, your anger then begins to transform into what I call wholehearted hatred, the next ingredient in a wholehearted protest.

What is wholehearted hate?

I know you're probably thinking, *could hate really be the answer?*

Yes. Yes, it can. Remember, what creates change? Hating something so much that you'll do whatever it takes to get a different result.

For those who think you hate nothing and that hate could never be the answer, bear with me and trust this process. I promise it's necessary. Consider for once that it may just be your apathy, avoidance, or fear that is stopping you from what you want most. If you consider yourself more of a natural hater—you've got plenty of hating going on—this will be more about *processing and healing* your anger to turn it into wholehearted hatred, so you can approach this from more of a wholehearted position.

Wholehearted hate is *processed* anger. It's *healed* anger. This gives you a new, heightened perspective. It means you've walked down the path of your own healing journey enough to look back and be able to see, "Yuck! Gross! That was awful. That living hell was trapping me and keeping me from my dreams, purpose, and the life I've wanted to live. I hate that those lies kept me from having what I want. I hate it so much that now, *now*, I am going to do something about it, so neither I nor anyone else has to walk that path again." This is where you begin to see purpose in the midst of the pain. No longer are you holding onto the anger of the past but instead, hope for your future. It's fueled by empathy and faith rather than resentment and fear. This perspective allows you to take the pressure off of the people, the things, and the experiences that caused you pain, and it puts your attention on the bigger picture. This is what drives action because now you're ready to create change, you're ready to *be* the change. This place of action now becomes the starting line for your own protest. A protest that began with processed pain, transformed into wholehearted hatred, and is guided by divine love.

What is divine love?

"My command is this: Love each other as I have loved you" (John 15:12).

How much does He love us? When we recognize that there is no greater love to be expressed than the willingness to lay down your life for another, which is exactly what Jesus did, you see how much He really loves us. *That* much. The Bible says His love is unfailing; it never ends. It's said to be agape love, which is the highest form of love. It is patient and kind, not envious or boastful, not arrogant or rude. It's not irritable or resentful. I mean, need I say more? Probably...

Divine love means living *from* love, not *for* love. When you walk in divine love, you realize how loved you already are. The Bible says, "Though the mountains be shaken and the hills be removed, yet my unfailing love for you will not be shaken nor my covenant of peace be removed" (Isaiah 54:10). This means you no longer need anyone or anything else to affirm you in order to feel more loved because you know that you already are. You don't have to earn it, you don't have to do more to get more, you don't have to accomplish more, achieve more, or be more to have more of His love. It already is. When you understand this sort of love, your life reflects it by no longer executing *for* love; you execute *from* love. This is divine love.

This means that starting a wholehearted protest is not about hating people. We spend way too much time throwing our aggression, blame, and judgments at other people. Believe it or not, people are not the issue. The issue is the mindset, and the more we execute from divine love, the more we can begin to see mindset patterns within ourselves and other people. It's easy to *think* people are the issue because people are an easy target, especially when we're on "opposite sides of the field," but people are not the problem. The problem is really the mindset. The problem is the worldview that is developed between the ages of five and eight and then reinforced for the next twenty-plus years. The problem is the pain that hasn't been processed, and the problem is all the unconscious habits that have turned viral. As you saw in your own life, before becoming conscious of your own limiting belief, it was unconsciously managing your decisions. When you really stand in a place of divine love, you'll begin to embody empathy, which allows you the ability to understand and share the feelings of another.

Now, I will also say loud and clear that this does not justify people's behaviors or choices in any way. I will not disagree with you that there are some sick people out there. Literally, sick of mind, body, and emotions who are making horrific, radically wrong, and inhuman decisions. I am *not* overlooking that in any way, shape, or form. I am not suggesting that we shouldn't have systems, laws, and customs in place that keep those who make wrong decisions in check. However, all it does do is point to the root issue versus the fruit of the issue. We can be mad at the person all day long, but when you understand the mindset or the mentality of that person, you gain leverage, and leverage is key to change. After all, you do want change, don't you?

You and I cannot control the habitual wrong that mindsets of other people are creating. But, with enough commitment, intentionality, and divine love, right here, right now, we can lean in together to create a better life for you and a better experience for those around you. We can begin doing our part to put a stop to the wrongful decisions that are being made around us by the stance we are willing to take. This is our place of purpose.

What is insane clarity of purpose and passion?

In trusting this process, I guarantee you will be creating a man or woman of fire, passion, and purpose who can begin building the life you dream of despite the excuses, reasons, mindsets, and people who are only less informed than you, without hurting anyone, but rather helping yourself and those within your sphere of influence. That's what this is all about. When you decide to do things with processed pain, out of wholehearted hatred, and in divine love, your influence increases, and you suddenly become the light on the top of the hill that our world so desperately needs. What am I suggesting? I am suggesting that with enough lights turned on, we light up this whole world in a different way! You shine in purpose and passion.

Each of us is innately built to solve a problem in the world (that's a core principle of purpose), but if we aren't healed, we can't see the solution, only the problem, so we don't see the manifestation of our greatest purpose manifested in this world. We can spot the issues, see the problems, and easily point our finger at the things or people we disagree with, but that's about as far as we get. And then we wonder why things are so messed up; we wonder why we're not thriving. We wonder why our marriages, finances, relationships, businesses, and careers, are in shambles or just barely surviving. It's like we've got ourselves loaded with opinions, complaints, and prejudices but little progressive action, and then we've conditioned ourselves to expect someone else to fix it for us. We rely on the government. We point the finger. We downplay our ability to make the change. Or worst of all, we turn a blind eye. The reality is, those are the areas in your home, community, and world that are waiting for each of us to step up and create change. **The world is waiting for you and your solution**. Ultimately, who cares what someone else is going to do about it? The more important question is, *what are you going to do about it?*

That means, believe it or not, **you are the solution you seek**. That's why God created YOU. "For we are God's handiwork, created in Christ Jesus to do good works, which God prepared in advance for us to do" (Ephesians 2:10). When you're healed, you are an activist for change who not only stands for something (conviction) but also stands against something (protest). You see problems, and you *do* something about them. You see pain, and you bring healing. You see division, and you bring unity.

Well, that's telling, isn't it?! The minute we change the way we look at the people, problems, and circumstances we face and consider our judgments through a place of wisdom and greater understanding, we position ourselves to be change agents. But how do we do that? How do we take our judgments and do something good with them? Glad you asked!

My Protest Exercise

All protests begin with a judgment or criticism. It's the recognition by a group of people that things aren't being done in a way that is deemed to be fair, just, or right. Your wholehearted protest begins the same way, which means it, too, is birthed in judgment. It's only when those judgments begin to get away from us (unprocessed pain) that we find ourselves in trouble and if we're not aware of why we judge, we'll keep making the same mistakes repeatedly. Here is how I define it:

· ·

Wholehearted Protest =
a. The ability to stand against something.
b. The wisdom within the judgment.

· ·

Did you know that your judgment could actually come from a place of wisdom? Did you know that it could actually benefit the greater good? It could actually be an alert for opportunity. It could be an area where your conviction could shine, and your greatest limitless vision could be fulfilled *if* you can see it through that perspective. Yes, judgment left to itself for long enough, misguided, and fueled in anger and fear typically messes up people's lives. But judgment used in a different way, in wisdom, has the power to transform cities.

But how do we do that? How do we find *the wisdom within the judgment*? First, you have to understand what judgment is and why we do it.

The word judge in Greek is *krino*, which basically means to separate and assume power over. What's happening when we judge is that we are creating separation. Our judgment causes us to build these walls unconsciously between ourselves and other people. Then because we don't want to be alone in our judgment, we begin the gossip train, or we identify with a group of people who proves our judgment right. This only forges these weird alliances

177

between "us and them," causing us to believe that we are somehow assuming power over someone or something. Look at the way our world does religion, politics, social rights, even business. If you're not on the "right" side, you're on the "wrong" side.

In our defense, judgment is part of our early survival mechanisms as humans. It's been given to us to warn us and to signal danger. It's designed to protect us. If you think back centuries ago, we had tribes, we ate off the land, and we defended ourselves and our tribe members from predators and enemies. Now, as our society and culture has evolved and being that we are less cavemen-ish in our approach, the way we use our judgment should also change, but for most of us, it doesn't. Instead of physically protecting a tribe as we once did, we are emotionally protecting ourselves. We judge not to protect our livelihood or our pack, but instead, to protect our own ego. We judge to make someone else wrong so that we can feel right, to compartmentalize our world, create emotional safety for ourselves, feel better about ourselves and the way we choose to live our lives, and on and on. We're throwing judgments, slinging criticism, and spreading gossip. Ultimately this allows *us* to make a judgment about *someone else* to keep *ourselves* safe.

Obviously, there is a benefit in remaining physically safe but you don't have to live your life any longer trying to emotionally protect yourself. You don't have to make someone else "wrong" just so you can be "right." You don't have to be on guard, or try to assume power over, or feel as though you have to separate yourself to live your life. Instead you want to learn to find the wisdom within the judgment.

With that being said, we will start this process with a judgment, which means I am going to give you permission to light up your judgments, right here, right now, and then I'm going to show you how to find the wisdom within it by looking at things a bit more objectively. We'll begin by having you ask yourself this simple yet profound question: *Whom do you judge?*

Now, *really* think about this. This could be someone you used to know, currently know, have never met, someone who you repeatedly judge, or is just someone who exemplifies all that you can't stand in this life. It could range from "They kind of bug me" to "I literally couldn't be in the same room with her."

Now, some of you are sitting there thinking, "What!? I don't judge anyone." Not true. Of course you do, we all do. Think about it. It could be the barista at your local coffee shop this morning who always makes your coffee wrong. It could be your mother-in-law whom you love, but man, she just does this thing. It could be the president of the United States, but give me someone.

For those of you who are like, "Geez, where do I start? Let me count the ways!" Don't hold back; everybody you judge, write their names down! Have at it. Who do you judge? Write their name(s) here:

_____

_____

_____

From there, I want you to write about all the reasons *why* you judge them here (get it all out … consider this more like therapy than discrimination):

_____

_____

_____

Of the entire list, whether you wrote down one hundred reasons or four, identify the top two or three reasons you judge this person or this group of people. Circle those reasons.

From there, I want you to take the path least traveled and take that person and all of the emotional charges you feel just thinking about them out of the equation—literally remove their face from your mind. I want you to consider a different perspective, just for a minute. Think about this person, this human, who does "these things" that you judge, and consider this: What is the *real* reason this person acts in this way? *Why* do they do what they do? What do they believe about themselves that makes them so "arrogant," "manipulative," "harmful," "self-conscious?"

For just a minute, I'd like you to consider the idea that "the thing" is rarely, almost never "the thing" but rather, *the thing under the thing*. If you remember back to belief formation and why we make the decisions we make, we aren't actually dealing with what we think we're dealing with, but rather unconscious emotions, thought patterns, belief systems, and habits. If we stopped shooting darts, we'd maybe see clearly enough as to what is really going on beneath the surface. So bottom line, my question is, what belief drives this person to act this way? Empathetically, consider the answer.

Let me give you an example. My friend Jordan did this work with me, and here was her answer:

"My mom is the person I judge the most. She drives me nuts. She is extremely manipulative, believes her own lies, and is just so fake. I can't depend on her, I don't believe her, and I feel out of control every time I'm around her. "

When I asked Jordan if she'd consider looking at her mom through a different perspective (and through the lens I am suggesting for you), she was open. "What is *the thing under the thing* that causes your mom to act this way?" I asked.

Jordan got tears in her eyes. "I don't know! Who could ever act this way, especially to their own daughter?" The pain is real. The judgment is real. That goes for all of us. We are not negating that with this work we're doing.

I replied, "I know, Jordan. This exercise does not make your mom right. It does not excuse her behavior. All we're trying to do is to set you free with the truth behind her actions, so you don't have to carry the weight of the judgment. Now, what type of belief causes someone to be fake, to lie to their own daughter, and to manipulate?"

Jordan looked up with tears in her eyes, "Well, this is someone who is hiding something. It's someone who is very afraid. They don't know who they are, so they lie."

"Agreed," I said.

Jordan said, "She lacks self-worth."

Bingo. Her mother's actions are steeped in unworthiness.

It does *not* make her mother's decisions okay. It does not make her wrongdoings right, but it does put some context around *why*. Her mother manipulates, lies, and throws people under the bus because her level of unworthiness is so high. That is exactly what Jordan can't stand because her conviction is to "live unapologetically YOU!" Jordan's mom cannot "live unapologetically YOU" because she believes she's unworthy, and it's the area that Jordan can't stand. She stands for "living unapologetically YOU" (conviction), and she passionately stands against unworthiness (protest)! Do you see that? It's not her mom she hates; it's unworthiness she hates.

Your turn. I will ask you the same thing I asked Jordan. Are you willing to look at this person from a slightly different perspective, *not* for their sake but for *yours*? If so, "What is *the thing under the thing* that causes this person to act this way?" Write your answer here:

_____

_____

_____

Bingo! And just like Jordan, hopefully, you can see what is really bothering you. Sure, this person bothers you, and sure, you don't like that they are "manipulative" or "condescending" or "controlling" or "passive-aggressive." I get it, but what you really don't like is the lack of self-esteem, the mediocrity, or the limitations that they are executing from. That's what you hate. This should cause you to feel passion arising within you. Do you feel it? Go ahead and write your protest below.

I passionately protest:

_____

_____

_____

Your answer is likely a good notice and, there's a reason that your judgment against this person is so harsh. Can I tell you why? And you promise not to hate me? Or throw this book off a cliff?

The book of Matthew says, "Why do you look at the speck of sawdust in your brother's eye and pay no attention to the plank in your own eye? How can you say to your brother, 'Let me take the speck out of your eye,' when all the time there is a plank in your own eye? You hypocrite, first take the plank out of your own eye, and then you will see clearly to remove the speck from your brother's eye" (Matthew 7:3–5).

The thing under the thing that we can't stand about someone else is the thing we can't stand about ourselves. It's the thing we struggle with ourselves. Now, you may not show up the same way that this person does. Jordan is *nothing* like her mom, in any way, but that beautiful, seemingly confident, hysterical, and outgoing girl, unfortunately, absolutely struggles with a lack of self-worth, so it's not her mom that she hates, but the lack of self-worth. She hates it so much because she knows what it does in her own life. She knows that every time she believes its lie, she can't live in her conviction of "live unapologetically YOU" because she is so worried about what other people think, so she's accommodating instead of really living.

For those of you who are courageous *and willing*, we have to ask ourselves this: Is the thing that this person struggles with also the thing I struggle with? They have low self-esteem; do I? They wrestle with mediocrity; do I? They set their own self-limitations; do I? Could it be that the thing I hate in someone else is also the thing I hate within myself? Ten out of ten times, the answer is yes.

At first, when you do this exercise, it can feel like turning that dagger around and pointing it back at yourself. But when you look a bit more closely, you'll find that you go from being angry to sad. Sure, we hate the manipulation, lies, and behavior it causes, but the "thing under the thing," the lack of self-worth, the inadequacy, or the mediocrity, that's the real issue, and that's what will make us sad.

Now just as we are using wisdom within our judgments toward other people, so are we to use it with ourselves. Judging yourself for low self-worth or mediocrity is only going to make it worse. But recognizing that the reason you're judging yourself is that "this thing" is also "the thing" that is stopping you from living 100 percent into your conviction is where we turn the heat up. This is where we build your hate. You don't hate this person. You don't hate yourself. You hate "this thing." You hate self-limitations, apathy, low self-worth, and mediocrity. You hate this thing for all the obvious reasons, but even more so, you hate it because now, hopefully, you can see, it stops *you* from living in your conviction. If you're not in your conviction, your limitless vision is not manifesting, and if that's not manifesting, it's likely that your limiting belief has got you tongue-tied. And it's also likely that your limiting belief is the culprit for this thing you protest. They all are tied together!

Look at my limiting belief as an example: "I am wrong. I am not important." This belief has created mediocrity in all areas of my life. Mediocrity is my protest. I passionately protest mediocrity. My limiting belief drives mediocrity because when I'm executing from this place, I am not being honest with myself. I am mirroring the people around me to avoid their judgment. I am busy spinning my wheels, mitigating the risk of being judged versus just being who I am because when I'm in my limiting belief, I don't want to be abandoned, so I show up half-ass and that, I hate! But it wasn't until I fully understood this that I was able to take the heat off of myself and those around me and recognize that the place of pain—mediocrity—was not something I wanted to spend my time judging but was instead a problem I was born to solve! That changed everything because, over time, my judgment dropped, and I was able to see clearly enough to build a life and a business around passionately protesting mediocrity. Do some people think I'm too much? Yep. Do some people think I'm too deep? Absolutely. But here's the deal, I can't live my life based upon what other people think. I have to build my life upon what I believe to be true for me, which is to stand for *Living Free* (my conviction statement) and to *Passionately Protest Mediocrity* (my protest statement).

In doing this exercise, we not only free ourselves, but we also give other people the opportunity to be freed. We break down the walls that separate us, and we begin to see that we all struggle with so many of the same core issues. Sure, how we choose to behave may look dramatically different, but the core is the same. When we judge the surface, we mistake the real issue. Could it be that both arrogance and avoidance are both birthed in low self-worth? From what I've learned, yes. Could it be that both control and people-pleasing are birthed in feeling inadequate? Unfortunately, yes. Could it be that both overcompensating and under compensating come from fear? Yes, absolutely. So yes, we can attack the results all day long, pointing fingers, shooting blame, lighting up our streets in protests of rage, *or* we can do what only we can do which is to heal. When we heal our own areas of inadequacy, low self-worth, and fear (or whatever it might be for you) we have the capacity to help someone else because we have "a full tank." It's hard to help someone if you haven't helped yourself, or as they say when flying a plane, "Put on your oxygen mask first before helping someone else."

Understanding your area of protest is so important because just like forgiveness, you don't do it for the sake of the other person; you do it for your own sake! When you learn that about real forgiveness and what it does to the soul, your world opens up. If someone has harmed you or hurt you, you don't forgive them to help them; you forgive them to help you. The same goes for the people and things you can't stand or that you judge. You're not doing it to let them off the hook. You're doing it to let yourself off the hook so you can start your own healing journey. You do it because it's good for you! Sure, it's a "new muscle," it's uncomfortable, and you have to face crazy emotions, but as always, let me ask you: What's the alternative?!

How do I utilize my protest in day to day life?

Believe it or not, the recognition and use of your protest will continue to heal you, day in and day out. If you really unpack Matthew 7:3–5, it shows us where our greatest place of purpose is as it pertains to our protest and will be the backbone of how we use it. It says, "…first take the plank out of your own eye, *and then* you will see clearly to remove the speck from your brother's eye" [emphasis mine]. Once you begin to "remove the plank from your own eye," you're going to automatically position yourself to have the ability and the capacity to support somebody else in doing the same. That means you're going to have to notice when the thing you protest is showing up in your life.

Step 1: Awareness. Awareness is key in this department. It is really hard to create change when you are not aware. I'll even say real change is *impossible* when you're not aware, so in order to use your protest every day, you're going to need to be aware of it, in yourself and in other people. Remember, the goal is to be consciously incompetent until you're consciously competent.

When you feel *yourself* making decisions from a place of avoidance, over-activity, mediocrity, unworthiness—whatever your protest may be— notice it. You have to see it happening. It'll be a jolt within you. Your heart may pound. You may feel butterflies in your stomach. You may feel spikes of anger, frustration, sadness, and fear. These things are just triggers that are alerting you to pay attention and recognize what's going on. It means there is still something within you that hasn't healed, and remember, our aim to wholehearted protesting is to heal and process our pain, to "remove the plank from our own eye first," so we can remove the speck of sawdust from someone else's. When you do see your area of protest arising to the surface, immediately say, "It's time to heal!"

The same is true for other people, so when you notice yourself judging someone else, take a step back, and consider the thing you judge in them is the thing you judge in yourself. When someone else is executing from a place of low self-worth, fear, mediocrity, doubt, or whatever your protest is, you've got to first consciously acknowledge that the reason this person "catches" you, "triggers" you, or just makes you so dang angry or frustrated is because they carry the same false truth that you do. Notice it for what it is. Internally, call it what it is and then empathize with it. I literally want you to say in your mind, "Me too!" I don't want you to cast judgment. I don't want you to fight back. I don't want you to avoid that person or the situation. I don't want you to throw blame or anger. I just want you, in your head and in your heart, to acknowledge what is going on and to dismantle its power by saying, "Me too!"

Remember, the "speck they have in their eye" is the speck you are here to remove. The more you heal in your own life, the more you'll be able to wholeheartedly stand against it. It's where your pain is given purpose. You will notice it, you will see when someone is struggling with it, but instead of reacting, you will proactively take your place of purpose and *do* something about it. And that, my friend, is a beautiful place to be!

I first recognized these flair ups within myself early on in my coaching career (thank God). Prior to understanding it or being able to acknowledge it in my everyday life, I would see people settling in areas of their lives. I would notice people justifying and giving excuses for everything that was happening in their lives, and it would piss me off. Internally, I felt like I was a time bomb. It wasn't until I realized that I, too, was still struggling with my own areas of settling, justifying, and excuse-giving that I was able to bring change about in my own life. I began to "go to work." Every time I noticed it in someone else, I would turn that judgment into wisdom, and I would take note of any additional residue of mediocrity showing up in my own life and I would do my part to continue healing. Over time, I was able to recognize the spirit of mediocrity in other people without the unnecessary flare ups because I had let the healing take place within me. Do you know what that did? It set me up perfectly to bring the solution to the problem I was seeing. I was able to approach my clients, friends, and family with so much more ease and grace. I was now on their side, working against mediocrity instead of standing on the other side, working against them. This is where I learned that people weren't the issue. The issue was the spirit of mediocrity that was robbing from the people I loved most. *That* made me mad. That ignited my reverent hatred. And I grew stronger and stronger.

Step 2: Grab the counterpart. Once you can spot the thing you protest in your life or the lives of others, the next step is to grab the counterpart, your conviction. So yes, you could cast judgment, throw daggers, assign blame, and lash out in your anger, *or* you could grab your conviction of "Live true," "Ride the ride that makes you proud," "Live unapologetically," or "Be the fire." You break the pattern with the juxtaposition. You break the pattern by flipping the coin. You will successfully stand *against* something because you courageously stand *for* something. That's the sweet spot.

What this does is dismantle the effects of your protest. Brené Brown talks about this in relation to shame. Shame makes us want to run and hide, protect ourselves, and even cover up our error, but truth be told, those behaviors will never rid us of shame. In fact, they will only make it worse. The way you dissolve shame is to shine light on it. You acknowledge it. You bring it out into the open because it cannot survive there. This is a gutsy move, don't get me wrong, and having struggled with shame for the first twenty-five years of my life, it was one of the harder things I had to do, but gosh darn it, I wouldn't be honest if I didn't admit that it worked like a charm. Every time I would feel the grip of shame, instead of falling into the area I protest (mediocrity), I would bring it into the light with my conviction of "live free." I would air its "dirty laundry." I would acknowledge it every single time I felt it, and over time, it lost its power over me. I proved to myself its illusion and therefore got my life back again. Your protest is no different; the more you air its dirty laundry and don't hide it away, the more you disempower its existence. But it will take guts, and guts you do have because if you remember, guts come from your conviction. Your conviction is your non-negotiable commitment, the thing you can't *not* do because it's God-ordered. You've got guts! You can do this!

Step 3: Do something about it. If we use our Dream Tree analogy, your protest, like your conviction, is a part of your root system. When you stand against fear (your protest) with love (your conviction), when you stand against a lack of self-worth (your protest) with gratitude (your conviction), when you stand against negativity (your protest) with hope (your conviction), you are gaining more strength in your root system. Ultimately, over time, belief by belief, step by step, you're building your limitless vision everywhere you go in everything you do.

When you identify something or someone you judge, instead of building walls, separating yourself, or beginning a gossip train, here are a few questions I would like for you to consider:

1. Is this triggering me to show me that I have an area in my life I need to heal? (The answer is likely yes, so you will need to take the necessary steps to heal.)

2. Is this also an issue I am wired to solve? (Consider your conviction. If yes, then this is the path to your own healing, to giving your pain purpose.)

3. Am I *willing* to do something about this?

    a. If so, then what are two things that I am committed to doing today that prove to myself (and even those around me) that I am serious?

    b. If not, am I willing to *shut up* about it? Am I willing to commit to making no more verbal judgments or criticisms about it and get on with my life?

Once you realize that the things you judge are a chance to heal and a pathway for greater purpose, the world opens up to you. You don't feel like you're walking around broken or stuck anymore. Now you're no longer victim to someone else's behavior. You don't have to sit in the seat of insanity, getting the same stuff, different day. You have a way to overcome nearly anything as long as you commit and apply yourself.

It's time to rise up and stand against "the thing under the thing." It's time to drop the judgments and to focus on the area you are built to solve, to bring change to any area of your life, family, career, community, and even the world!

If you're ready, commit here:

I, _____, commit to purposefully and
         (name)

passionately stand against _____.
                            (protest)

I will live honestly in my conviction,_____,
                                  (conviction)

and I commit to no longer complaining, blaming, or gossiping about the

issues that I'm not willing to do something about. I will DO something

about them. I will be a change agent for the greater good to see my vision

come to pass, _____!
                  (limitless vision)

_____
        (signature)

You are called to
live your life
standing against
the issues that are
not in alignment
with what
God is doing.

SECTION 3

LIVING TO CREATE

CHAPTER 11

What are You Dreaming? Becoming a Conscious Creator

LOOK HOW FAR YOU'VE COME. I bet you didn't think this book was going to offer you all this insight, did you?! Perhaps it is even a little deeper than you thought it was going to be?! Yeah, I get that a lot. You just thought you were picking up some "woo-woo," make-you-feel-good book on dreaming, didn't ya?! Ha!

Dreaming can be a tricky concept because, in theory, we all like the *idea* of dreaming, but few of us really understand the actual responsibility it requires. It requires *all* of us! It requires you to heal and to go deeper than perhaps you've ever gone before because dreaming is radically in tune with a different dimension. It requires you tuning in to higher levels of awareness, authenticity, and alignment within yourself. It requires a better understanding of your own self-imposed limits (limiting beliefs) and mind chatter. It requires a better understanding of what you stand for and what you stand against. It requires a better understanding of growth tools not only to obtain our dreams but also to sustain them. It requires a better understanding of vision. It requires deeper insights into God and His word. All of which you have done! I mean, come on now, you've done the work, my friend, good job!

But, as promised, the whole goal of this book is to help you identify your dreams so that you can unapologetically chase those dreams, so let's get on with it, shall we?! It's time to dream!

As mentioned early on in Chapter 1, I explained my definition of the word dreaming as:

* *

Great and intense focus, with deep absorption
of thought, in a different realm that brings
about possibilities while considering the
needs of those around you.

* *

Here in these last few chapters, I will help you get laser clear on the dreams you hold within you so you can begin crafting your life around those dreams. We are going to take what's in you and get it out of you! And I'm not talking about any ol' dream; I'm talking about your piece of heaven that you are destined and designed and purposed to bring to this earth. I'm talking about the kind of dream that is so much bolder, purer, and more profound than your own head could ever imagine. The kind of dream "no eye has seen, no ear has heard, and no human heart has conceived" (1 Corinthians 2:9, Christian Standard Bible*). The kind of dream that your life was born to create, the dream that heaven specifically designed for you to release to a world that so eagerly awaits in expectation.

Now, for any of you who may have bits and pieces of a skeptic still in you, let me start this section by prefacing it with an interesting fact. Research has shown that your brain doesn't know the difference between reality and imagination. What does that mean? It means that if you can imagine it, you can *have* it! This is why we want to ensure your dreams are as real, clear, aligned, and authentic as possible because you're powerful enough to create whatever it is you can imagine. So be careful, little heart, what you see. The good news is, after all the work you've done, you have the foundational pieces to create from a place of limitless vision, conviction, and a whole heart, which will help to clarify and shape your most real, purest, and wildest dreams.

Let me start by asking you a series of questions to get your juices flowing:

What would the world look if your limitless vision *was* manifested in the world around you? What would you be doing more of or less of? What's possible for you when you're living in your vision? What's possible for other people? What would be inspiring you? What would motivate you? What dreams would come from this vision?

What would your life look like if you were living in your conviction? How would you show up on a day to day basis? Where would you be spending your time? What would become more important to you, and what would become less important to you? What dreams would come from this conviction?

What would your life look like if you were passionately and unapologetically standing in your protest without fear or judgment? What would you be doing? What would you not be doing? What dreams would come from this protest?

What would heaven on earth look like? What would be happening around you, in your life, family, career, and community? What would be going on within you? What would be possible for you? What would be possible for other people?

I'm not just asking you these questions rhetorically. They do deserve actual answers, and I will ask you to put pen to paper, but first, you must get clear.

Clarify

For most, if we're honest, we're not clear in a lot of different areas in our lives, let alone our dreams and goals. We know what we *don't want*. We know what our neighbors have that we *think* we should have. We know what's possible based upon what we can currently see, but that's not very motivating to most of us. Hence our lack of action and the one burning question that every dreamer-in-waiting has: *Is there something more?*

So if we all want clarity on our dreams, why are so few actually clear? Before we get clear, I think it's important to understand why we stay unclear. Believe it or not, we stay unclear because it's giving us something. Even though we admit we don't like being unclear, it's benefitting us somehow; otherwise we wouldn't hang onto it. So for those of you who are unclear, I'd like you to ask yourself: What is my lack of clarity giving to me?

The first reason we stay unclear is to be right. Look, we all want to be right because nobody wants to be wrong. This goes back to our limiting beliefs. If we have a belief that says, "Nobody loves me" or "I can't have what I want," then the goal of my ego is to prove that to be true so I can be what? Right!! Blech! How awful is that? So, if I start to build relationships with people who love me, and I start chasing the dreams within me, the things I really want, then according to my above belief, I'd be wrong. And since nobody wants to be wrong, I'll likely sabotage my own progress. It's important to recognize during this clarity phase that you need to continue to ask yourself: *Do I want to be right, or do I want to be clear?* At all costs, avoid trying to be right. Remind yourself you want to be clear!

The second reason we stay unclear is that we do not want to take responsibility for what we're about to find. If I know my answer, I have to do something with it. If I know what I want, then I have to do something about it.

That can feel vulnerable, intimidating, and, of course, uncomfortable, so if we aren't conscious of this, we will stay in the land of ambiguity. We'll hide behind three of the most devastating, dream-killing words: "I don't know." As long as I don't know, I'm not responsible. I'm not responsible for what I have to do next. I don't have to put myself out there. I don't have to ask for help. I don't have to start over. I don't have to quit. I don't have to admit failure. I don't have to trust God (or myself) and on and on. Let's face it, being responsible is hard—no doubt about it. But so is not being clear. May I remind you, given the two options, pick the *hard* that is going to serve your most real, purest, wildest dreams. I am a firm believer that we always know. We may not know at first thought, but we *always* know. The answer to most of our life's questions, concerns, obstacles, and issues resides on the inside of us. God put insight and wisdom inside each of us for a reason, but most haven't refined the gift or learned how to tune in enough to hear ourselves because we've used the cop-out reason of "I don't know" to let us off the hook. Clarity forces your hand, and it requires responsibility.

The third reason we remain unclear is to stay comfortable. Learning something new, chasing after our dreams, doing what we've never done pushes us into the world of the unknown. And that can be scary. We don't know it, we don't get it, we can't compartmentalize it, and ultimately, it blows our mind. In honor of your greatest, yet to be fulfilled dreams, let it. Let it blow your mind and resist the urge to stay comfortable. You have to, have to, have to get uncomfortable. It's in the land of discomfort that everything you want awaits you. I promise you it won't kill you.

As you can see, we have every reason, or at least three reasons, to stay unclear, but you also have every dream to get clear. It's hard to get clear, but it's also hard to be unclear. It's hard to tune in to yourself, but it's also hard to be so tuned in to everyone else that you lose yourself in the process. So may this be your friendly reminder that yes, getting clear is hard, *and* it's likely a better hard to choose.

Now that we understand a few of the reasons we stay unclear, let's look at how we become more clear. I've learned that it's less about knowing how to become clear and more about just the practice of creating space to be clear, so what I'm going to ask you to do is create the space *and* "go in."

When I say "create space *and* go in," what I mean is creating an environment around you and within you that enables you to tune in to yourself and the spirit of God that's leading you, while tuning out the rest of the world. It's about blocking out all the noise—the excuses, the reasons, the judgment, the opinions of others, your past, future, fear, doubt, worry, and justification, and just going quiet with yourself. Because, when was the last time you did that?

My point exactly.

So first things first, I am going to ask you to create space in any way you can. Go to your favorite place in your home or go outside and find your favorite beautiful view, anywhere that provides the peace and serenity you need to clear your mind and be still. It's likely that you are going to have to intentionally block out time on your calendar to do this. You can do this early morning before the day's hustle and bustle begins, at the end of your day before you go to sleep, during your lunch break, or even in your car between meetings. You must learn to create the space because it won't create itself.

I love that the Bible says, "The Lord is my shepherd, I lack nothing. *He makes me* lie down in green pastures, *he leads me* beside quiet waters, he refreshes my soul. *He guides me* along the right paths for his name's sake" (Psalm 23:1–3 [emphasis mine]). Those are very sit your butt down, proactive statements. "*He makes me* lie down … *he leads me*." Why? Because could it be that if He doesn't make us lie down and rest that we'll miss the still waters? By not doing this, we miss the opportunity to "go in." Regardless, you and only you are responsible for creating this space. No, it's not going to come easy at first. No, it doesn't happen on its own accord. It's something we must be intentional about. And no, you're not too busy. Even in the Bible, there are countless mentions where even Jesus had to proactively withdraw to a solitary place to be with God. The bottom line, if Jesus could do this, as busy as He was, so can you.

Once you're in your space, you will begin the process of "going in." This is meditation. This is the art of sitting still, quietly, by yourself. When you meditate, "go in," you are changing the brain because the prefrontal cortex actually shuts off. This is the part of the brain that holds your mental chatter. As mentioned early on in the book, research has shown that these meditative states lower anxiety, stress, and angst because we are literally turning off the parts of the brain that create unchecked thought processes, resulting in misaligned emotions. That's why, when you're in these quiet, meditative states, you will find that you're finally able to hear your own heart, and not because it wasn't speaking before but because you are still enough to hear it. You might not have heard your own voice before because it is simply too kind to compete with all the other noise. It will stay still until you are.

More importantly, this also helps to realign you with the source of your wisdom and strength. "Look to the Lord and his strength; seek his face always" (1 Chronicles 16:11). "Call to me and I will answer you and tell you great and unsearchable things you do not know" (Jeremiah 33:3). "This is the confidence we have in approaching God: that if we ask anything according to his will, he hears us" (1 John 5:14). It's in these quiet moments of "going in" that you align with the very heart of God; you hear Him speak. You capture His voice about your dreams.

I have found three layers to this process—I call these the chatter layer, the constructive layer, and the creation layer. When I sit down to "go in," I first approach my chatter layer. This is usually a rather disruptive, awkward five to fifteen minutes. My mind is going crazy. Like the top of my head, where my brain is, actually feels like it is on fire. It's screaming to be heard, vying for my attention, and like the painful process of someone going through withdrawal, it's really loud and distracting. The enemy knows the power of this quiet place, and the last thing he wants you to do is to get quiet with yourself and with God because he knows that when you know, you are an unstoppable force. Lean in even more. This is normally where I journal and pray and just kind of unload the weight of it all. I write and I write and I write, I pray and I pray and I pray until I just run out of things to say. And believe me, you will run out of things to say. The chatter subsides and the thoughts that try to distract you from God's purpose in your life eventually stop.

The second layer is where I open my journal to a fresh page because it is beyond the psycho chatter layer and becomes rather constructive. I'm not yet in a heartfelt layer, but I do come up with some pretty cool ideas. This is the layer where I suddenly remember to call someone I forgot. I come up with a great branding idea. I think of a cool Bible story I want to tell my kids. I'm reminded of past ideas and strategies that I haven't put into action yet. For me, this is a progressive state, so I capture the thoughts and reminders it brings to me, and I jot them all down on a piece of paper with no additional planning or energy. Just write it down and let it be. This layer can take five minutes, or it can take fifteen but believe me, it, too, runs itself out, and once it does, you're "in."

The third layer is where I am "in." It is the creation layer. This is the heart phase, where my ego is not allowed. It's not about being right or wrong, it's not about the can and cannots, and it's way beyond any fear, worry, or ping of doubt I could experience. This phase is about the nudge, the gut feeling, the intuition, following the lead of my knowing, and hearing the voice of God speak to me and through me. Often at this phase, you'll see images and pictures, get a full download of insight, gain understanding you've never had before, tap into deeper levels of curiosity, and you'll begin to clarify your most real, purest, wildest dreams without any forced effort whatsoever.

We're funny because we think God should show up and talk to us in literal, practical ways as if He speaks our language, but God speaks in signs and wonders, with images and ideas that are so clearly not our own that we have no doubt where they came from. It's pure, gentle, subtle and a lot of times, even blank. In this level of creation, never hold yourself back from what you see, never criticize yourself or your imagination, don't compare, reason, or even ask "how." Stay true to what you find. Connect with yourself. Connect with God. Connect with your dreams.

Once this phase is done, again, this can last five minutes, or it can last thirty minutes, and I have seen all I need to see (even if that means nothing), I grab my journal for the third time. I encourage you to do the same. This is when I write down every single thing I saw, felt, noticed, and experienced. I write it all down, doing my best to leave nothing behind. I capture every last word, and I write the visions of my heart. Here's why. When you come out of this state, real life is going to hit you—mind chatter, distractions, reality, all the things. You are going to have to keep close to you the things that came to you while you were "in," so you can begin to manifest those when you are "out." You are going to have to hold the vision and trust the process.

I did have a coaching student say to me once, "I'm not as profound and deep as you. I mean, I'm a tactical guy, and I need more of a 1-2-3-step guide to meditating and talking to God." Oh Lord, in heaven, I thought. This proves my point exactly. We don't need a 1-2-3-step guide because that would defeat the purpose. Just as a relationship with a husband and wife is unique and fashioned only for them, so is the relationship you have with yourself and with God. There is no other you, and there is no other relationship like the one you have with yourself and with God, which means, there is no 1-2-3-step guide.

"Well, how will I know when it's a dream? How will I know I am hearing God?" You practice. You practice, you practice, and you practice. Sometimes you won't recognize your own voice or even God's voice because you're so used to hearing everyone else's. Begin this process and let it be more about gaining familiarity than getting it right. It's about learning to trust yourself and trust His leading, and that will only come when you begin this process. Start your journey and reflect as you go. That's why this is a daily process. I once heard someone say that the goal of meditating is not to be good at meditating; the goal of meditating is to be good at you. The goal of "going in" is not to get it right. The goal of "going in" is to "go in." Don't do this just to be good at it. Don't do this just to check something off your to-do list. Do this because it's a practice in becoming a better version of you, a practice in hearing yourself, hearing your God, and hearing the deepest dreams within you.

"What if I don't hear anything in this quiet space?" This isn't always about hearing something every time you do it. Often it's about *knowing*. "It is the glory of God to conceal a matter; to search out a matter is the glory of kings" (Proverbs 25:2). What does that mean? It means that God is not keeping anything from you. It also doesn't mean He's not answering your prayers. It simply means that He is God, and you are not. It means that He wants to be in a relationship with you more than He wants to give you answers. It's an opportunity for you to want the healer more than the healing. If you understood everything, you wouldn't need God. This space is designed to build and develop intimacy between you and God and you and yourself.

Now it's your turn. Can you take the time, and can you create the space to "go in?" And when you do, consider revisiting the questions I asked you at the beginning of the chapter. They will lead you to finding answers. Also, consider the following questions:

What do I want most? What's most important to me? What will make me the most proud? If I wasn't afraid of being hurt again, what would I do? Even if I would be hurt or disappointed, what would I go after? If I felt loved and supported, how would I live my life? If I wasn't dependent on other people's approval, what would I do? If I no longer had to settle, what would I go after? What has God put on my heart? God, show me your heart. What do you want for me?

Continue by asking yourself: *Who do I want to be? What do I want to do (with my time and my career)? What do I want to have? What do I want to give (to people and this world as a whole)?*

When I'm in this place, a few additional ways I prompt myself to find my answers is to consider every area of my life that is deserving of my dreams. I call these my "live to thrive five," and it includes mind and spirit, health and well-being, relationships and environment, career, and finances. You can download this document for free at www.TheDreamFactoryandCo.com/livetothrive5. What would it look like to have a free mind and spirit? What would it look like to have vibrant health and well-being? What kind of relationships matter most to me? What kind of environment will cause me to thrive? What kind of career do I want to craft for myself for my own enjoyment and also for the enjoyment of others? What does it mean to live financially free?

All of these questions will give you many ways "in." Ask each question and surrender to the process. Don't judge the outcome. Don't rush the process. Be still and know.

Verify

Once you have spent some time clarifying your greatest dreams, the next step is to verify them. I want you to review every single item you wrote down. Look at what you've written down in awe and majesty of the joy, curiosity, passion, purpose, excitement, and inspiration it brings to you. Consider how beautifully handcrafted all of those dreams are. Thank yourself for the exercise, thank God for His revelation, and don't be afraid to keep adding to it. In fact, you should continue to add to it for the rest of your life because, let's be honest, you're never really done clarifying and manifesting your dreams as long as we're alive, which means that you will always be in pursuit of your dreams as long as you're breathing.

If all of that resonates, I want you to do one more thing with these dreams to verify them even more. I want you to go line by line with each of the dreams you wrote down and ask yourself (with a completed, written down answer): *WHY? Why do I want this dream? What is it about this dream that I want most? What is the result really going to give me? How will this dream benefit the people around me? What makes this dream so important to me? Are these dreams in alignment with my limitless vision? Are these dreams in alignment with my greatest conviction? Will they support me in standing against my greatest protest? And most importantly, Are my dreams in alignment with God's Word?* Your dreams should never contradict the written word of God.

I want you to really consider *why* you want these dreams because I want you to check your motivation behind each dream to recognize that it's not just about the stuff, the acquisition, or even the accomplishment for the sake of the accomplishment. It's more than that. It has to be. It's deeper than that. It has to be. I think that's why so many people burn out in pursuit of just chasing more accomplishments, stuff, and validation because, at some point, it's empty, and we long for more—purpose, meaning, and significance. If our dreams don't hold a deeper place within our heart and a connection point to heaven, we won't manifest them because consciously or unconsciously, it won't matter that much to us. The thing(s) will come and go. The money, the accolades, the house, the cars, the stuff, and even the name recognition, all of it will come, which means, all of it will also go. So, if you are not tied to something bigger than the thing, you will be psyched when it comes but then devastated when it goes or frustrated when it doesn't come easy and resentful when it doesn't last. "What good is it for someone to gain the whole world, yet forfeit their soul?" (Mark 8:36).

Here's what I've learned in my journey in pursuit of my own dreams, especially as I've accomplished a lot of what I wanted to accomplish in the first part of my life. **The dream is not just about the dream. The goal is not just about the goal. It's about who you become in the process.** We give so much weight to the accomplishment and achievement that we begin to convince ourselves that "once I achieve that, have that, earn that, or buy that, then I will be happy. Then I will be fulfilled. Then I will feel complete, validated, loved." We think that it's all about the accomplishment, the achievement, or the acquisition, but there's so much more to it than just that. Now, I'm not suggesting that the accomplishment of these dreams and every goal isn't going to feel and be amazing. The endorphins resulting from accomplishment are great, but they can be rather addictive if we're not careful, and all of a sudden, we begin to think that the stuff, the acquisitions, and the accomplishments are necessary to feel fulfilled in this life, and like a drug, it will run us into the ground. However, the achievement of the dream is not just about the dream. The goal is not the goal. It's *who you become on the way to achieving your dreams and goal* that is where all the good stuff is made. Believe me, you won't care if you gain the whole world if you lose your soul.

When you execute from a deeper place of *why*, when you're chasing something that is completely in alignment with your limitless vision and conviction, you will begin to notice that you execute *from* love, joy, passion, and purpose, not *for* it. When you recognize that you have what you need on the inside of you already, even the fulfillment of your dreams and goals doesn't make you better or worse because you're not tied to them. The accomplishment doesn't give you a better identity. You've already got an identity that you love and appreciate; therefore you can't help *but* accomplish the things that are important to you. The accomplishment of that dream just means that your identity came out of you. And *that* is what will feel good, to see all of you manifested in the world around you.

By verifying what you wrote down, you're spot-checking yourself to ensure your dreams are real, pure, and wild to *you*. You do not want to spend extra energy pursuing things that are outside of the will of God for your life or are only to fuel your ego, or make you feel valued for a moment. You want to ensure all of you and all of heaven is embodied in all of your goals and dreams. From there, it's time to start visualizing!

Visualize

Visualization is the next step to manifesting your dreams. It is completely underestimated, partially because we've watered it down and partially because we don't actually understand how to use it. Visualizing is about learning how to create new mental images of possibilities and dreams. Just as getting clear is a practice of forgetting about the *how* and instead tapping into the *why*, visualization is a practice that supports you in etching the pictures of your dreams into the very fiber of your being, which enables you to *embody your dreams before they exist*. That means visualization is not about *feeling* good but rather growing familiar with where your dreams are about to take you before you even get there.

Here's why this is so dang important. When you begin the process of becoming clear of your greatest dreams, though they are beautiful and important, they are also unknown to you. Whether you dream of writing a best-selling book, starting a business, becoming an activist or a missionary, losing thirty pounds and living your healthiest life, having an intimate, loving relationship, traveling the country in an RV, or whatever it might be, you've never actually achieved those dreams before and they can feel very unfamiliar. Because they are so unfamiliar, they can also feel very uncomfortable. Depending on your threshold for being uncomfortable, you might be unconsciously in resistance to your own dreams, not because you don't *want* them to manifest but because you actually don't *know* or *understand* them. This can cause you to feel unsafe, and our tendency is to avoid anything that doesn't make us feel safe, be it literal or emotional.

This is why far too many of us are not accomplishing our dreams. It's not because we can't; it's because we don't feel safe in doing so. Our dreams live in a world we do not understand—they blow our minds—therefore unconsciously, we don't feel safe, and no one likes to do anything they don't feel safe doing. It's no freaking wonder we're not unapologetically chasing down our every heart's desire. It's why we aren't crushing our dreams. It's because we've never experienced them, so we don't actually feel safe pursuing them. If we did, we would run openheartedly and unapologetically towards them. Sure, having more money sounds great, but we don't know what our friends and family will think. We don't know how life would feel if we had more money. Sure, writing a book and impacting millions of readers sounds amazing, but we don't know what the process feels like or what to expect from editors, marketing, distribution, and readership. Yes, losing thirty pounds and getting in the best shape of our lives is an amazing dream, but if we're honest, we have no clue what it will feel like or how we will even interact with ourselves, let alone other people. So if we don't approach this process consciously, we may start but shy away or simply won't start at all because it's not familiar to us, *not* because it's impossible.

Visualization takes this dream of yours and begins the process of familiarizing itself within you. Every time you sit down and envision the life you want and the dreams you have, what you're actually doing is giving yourself the opportunity to feel safe and secure with something you have yet to accomplish. By doing this often enough and with enough frequency, your head and your heart literally begin to feel safe. The minute we feel safe, our guard comes down, and we have fewer reasons *not* to do something, so we do! The more you visualize something, literally taking the time to embody it, feel it, and see it in your mind's eye, the more familiar it becomes, and the more familiar something becomes, the easier it is to obtain because we feel safe in having it! The art of visualizing is great because it requires you to continue to produce clarity for your heart and soul (which it needs) while also producing safety and security for your head (which it needs). Game changer y'all!

Now, I'd like you to review your greatest dreams, but this time, I want you to close your eyes, and I want you to actually *feel* your dreams. I want you to feel what it feels like to embody them. I want you to feel yourself manifesting your dreams. I want you to feel yourself en route to those dreams. I want you to feel the sensations in the body, watch where you light up, get comfortable with what you want. I want you to envision God and all the angels dancing over you as you chase your dreams. Give it a try, right here, right now.

I encourage you to continue doing this every single day. Just like you don't familiarize yourself with a new friend or a new city overnight, the same is true with your dreams. The longer you sit with them, the more real they will become, and ultimately, the more likely are you to manifest them in the world around you because you have grown so accustomed to them within you. I want you to *commit* to yourself that every day for as long as it takes to manifest these dreams that you will embody them and visualize them—be it for thirty seconds or thirty minutes. In this time of visualization, I want you to honor God, honor the dreams within you, honor your heart, and begin creating familiarity with every single one of your dreams. Maybe you picture one dream a day. Maybe you visualize a whole handful or the whole dang list every day. It doesn't matter. What I want you to do is commit to yourself that you are going to do this because it is the first action step, literally, emotionally, and mentally, toward everything that you want.

Note, as you go to do this, your unchecked thoughts will often chime in and fearfully ask: "But how?"

And you will immediately respond, "Thank you, but we don't need to know how yet. We are safe."

The unchecked thoughts will then ask: "But when?"

And you will immediately respond, "Thank you, but we don't need to know when just yet."

It will then continue with: "Who, what, where…??"

And you will follow with: "Yes. I hear you. Thank you. In due time."

Remember, the unchecked thoughts don't actually need to be right; they just want to be heard. As long as your head knows you won't die, it doesn't need a solid answer. It just needs to be assured that it's safe and you can continue on your merry way. Like meditation, visualization is not about being good at it, in and of itself, so do not go into this just trying to be good at it. The goal of this is to be a better you! Be sure you're not just trying to get good at it for the sake of getting good at it but rather doing it to "go in" and to become more in tune with your dreams and therefore on the path to accomplishing every dream you have.

Believe me, this will take some time to master (ask me how I know), and your head does deserve answers to all those questions, but the reality is, you don't know those answers *yet*. You will figure them out as you go. Jesus said, "Don't be afraid; just believe" (Mark 5:36). Don't try to plan out perfectly something that you cannot control. Instead, visualize the deepest desires you have within you, solidify your conviction, unapologetically chase your limitless vision, and let God be God. Let go of the things you cannot control and grab onto the One who holds the entire universe in the palm of His hands. The Bible says, "For we live by faith, not by sight" (2 Corinthians 5:7). We will not see the power of God if we do not step outside of our own control. By chasing your dreams, you are letting go of control and mental conditioning, and you are stepping into a walk of faith.

As we close out this chapter and shift into the action-oriented next chapter, here's one last thing I want you to consider as you reflect on your dreams and on clarifying, verifying, and visualizing them:

. . . .

Dream real, live big.

. . . .

We don't need more half-hearted dreams. We need wholehearted dreams. We need all of you in all of your dreams. Do you remember the little old lady, from the beginning of the book, who said life was getting in the way of her dreaming?! It's not that life was getting in the way; it's that she didn't have a dream bigger than her life to chase after. If you ever feel similarly, like life is getting in the way of your dreams, then I propose that your dreams aren't real enough. If they were, life would never stop you from chasing them. This is why your dreams need to be real because the more real they are, the bigger they become.

I am never an advocate for "dream big" just for the sake of having big dreams. That can easily be all about ego and the secret's out, whoever has the biggest dreams doesn't win an extra prize. However, I am a huge advocate for *real* dreams. And the irony, as mentioned, is that the more real your dreams are, the bigger they become. It's an automatic by-product. Once those dreams become real, they become big—real big, much bigger than you could ever manifest on your own accord or in your own strength or understanding. Quite the conundrum. But here's the real magic and the two reasons we want to dream real dreams that are bigger than us:

The first reason is to bring humanity together. As mentioned, your dreams are not just for your own benefit but also for the benefit of those around you. Remember, a dream "brings about possibilities while considering the needs of those around you." If we take one step further, your dreams will also *include* those around you. When you dream real dreams that are bigger than you, it automatically means you will need someone else to help you, and when we work side by side one another, for a cause and a reason that's bigger than ourselves, we come together as people.

When we just go to a job, sit at our desks, go home and do our life, share a few posts, hit a few "like" buttons, but aren't actually working together for the sake of a common goal, we aren't strengthening our bond with each other nor are we learning to trust each other. This causes us to build our lives apart from one another, which is why we're not seeing more "impossible" things become possible. In 1 Corinthians, the Bible is very clear about our giftings and working together as one. It says, "There are different kinds of gifts, but the same Spirit distributes them. There are different kinds of service but the same Lord. There are different kinds of working, but in all of them and in everyone it is the same God at work. Now to each one the manifestation of the Spirit is given for the common good" (1 Corinthians 12:4–7). We are all part of this body, and it is together we can fully manifest *for the common good.* Together actually means doing things in one accord and in unison with one another, not just for you, not just for me, but for the common good.

Now, I know we've each got a laundry list of disappointments and all the "times we've tried working together, and it didn't work." I've got my list too. But it doesn't mean that it doesn't work. Just because the mission failed once or twice or even 100 times doesn't mean it's impossible; it just means you found a few ways *not to do it,* which means you, of all people, should have a better understanding and insight of *how to do it.* Sure, you can protect yourself, live in a silo, and continue to dream dreams that only you can control, or you can take a bit of a risk and begin to dream more real dreams, which become bigger dreams, that will require the help of more people around you, all the while learning how to assess their heart for your dream. If you can begin to find the people who have the same heart, passion, and purpose for the things that you do, then it will be a better fit for everyone. But, in order to do that, in order to find those people, you're going to have to first dream dreams that are more real to you and then you're going to have to put those dreams out there so you can find the people who want to chase your dream with you. What if your dream is their dream too?

The second reason we should dream real is to bridge the gap between us and our Creator. Most people miss the opportunity we have in knowing God but when we begin to dream real dreams, it's as if we're opening up a door to heaven. If all our dreams are within our own strength, then we are solely dependent on ourselves. We don't need anyone or anything else. And cool, maybe that will fly for some time, but I guarantee, that will only be motivating for so long. It will also become rather exhausting because it all happens in the willpower zone, and ultimately, we do burn out.

I think the God we forget about, or simply don't know, is the One who wants your dreams to happen more than you do. We have a God who is a dreamer. We have a God who is a Creator. We have a God who wants to work with us to create the impossible. We have a God who is so much bigger, so much more capable and more able than we could ever be, and yet, our biases, judgments, and even prejudices around Him can distort the truth. Many have shared with me their bad experiences in a church growing up or a disappointment from a pastor or a situation that didn't happen the way they thought it should, and it built this barrier between them and God when in reality, He didn't do any of that. None of it. Yet we find ourselves asking questions like:

Well, why didn't God help me?

Why didn't God protect me?

Why didn't God step in and stop this bad thing from happening?

Where was God when …?

Why doesn't God answer my prayers?

All of those questions are fair, and honestly, we forget that we have a God who can hang with our hard questions. He can hang with your doubt. He can hang with our disbelief because He knows that if we stay there long enough and we lean in to understand, we will find more than just an answer. We will find Him.

But for most, we let our emotions take over, we shut down, and we make up conclusions about God. Here's the truth, our God is a God of freedom and free will. Just as we don't want to be God's robot, none of us want a God to tell us what to do, how to do it, or when to do it. We must be careful that we don't have expectations that He should at least fix all the problems, answer all our prayers the minute we pray them, and make everything "perfect and right" to fit into our plan and agenda. That, to me, doesn't seem to be a fair request or a mutually beneficial relationship. We want things to happen in our way, in our timing, in how we think they should happen (we want to play God), but then we point fingers, cast judgment, and blame God when things don't go our way. That doesn't feel like a healthy relationship. Yet that's what we do if we're not careful.

God is a God of free will and freedom, which means He gives *all* of us the room to make decisions. We all have a choice. And perhaps, instead of blaming God when things don't go our way or as planned, maybe we should thank Him for our free will and then honor the gift with better decision-making practices (as you've learned in this book).

By dreaming more real, you begin to recognize that your dreams can't happen in your own power or strength and that you need someone else, something bigger to support you in manifesting it. Yes, people will help, willpower will help, clarity and visualization, persistence, and getting a coach, all these things will help. AND I still believe the most untapped potential still awaits us in a heavenly realm. After all, who doesn't want an angel to have their back? Who doesn't want the Creator of the Universe (not just "the universe") to help them in obtaining their dreams? Who doesn't want a bigger power supporting them in their lifetime? Once you break it down, how's the alternative, without heaven, serving you?

Life is so much bigger than we could think it is. Life after this life is so much bigger than our minds could ever comprehend. What's possible is so much bigger than we think it is. Having real dreams is so much bigger than we could ever imagine and it's in having those real dreams that we become bigger (more real) people. It makes our connections with others deeper, and it makes our relationship with God so much more alive and authentic. We begin to do more out of faith and less out of doubt. We do more out of hope and less out of fear. We do more out of awareness and less out of avoidance. We *do* more because we *believe* more. That's a can't *not* win strategy if you ask me.

Dream real, live big!

DREAMING

is about creating an
environment around
you and within you that
enables you to tune out
the rest of the world so
you can tune into
yourself and the spirit
of God that's
leading you.

CHAPTER 12

Dreaming is a Verb—
Turning Dreamers into Doers

NOW THAT YOU'VE TAKEN THE TIME to get clear on your dreams, clarifying, verifying, and visualizing them, let's figure out the key component to manifesting those dreams. Here we go, ladies and gentlemen, it's the moment we've all been waiting for: "How do we make our dreams come true?"

The simple answer: *action*.

We *do* something. The only difference between your dreams and reality is called action.

Here's what I have found to be true about action, those who say "it's impossible" or "it can't be done" typically are those who haven't tried. Or, they've tried once or twice but given up. But those who make the "impossible," possible, and the "it can't be done," done, are those who *do* something (and don't stop). That's the only difference. They take massive action.

As mentioned, clarifying, verifying, and visualizing your dreams are incredibly powerful practices to manifesting your dreams, but in and of themselves, they will not change your life. You can clarify, verify, visualize, and even strategize all you want, but without *doing* something about your dreams, there will be no impact on your life. The impetus for change happens when we take action and *do* something with what we've learned. Information is cheap. *Applied* information is a game changer.

We live in what's called the Information Age. Anything we need is attainable with the click of a button, twenty-four seven. We can Google just about anything and either find the answer or, heck, a whole heap of opinions. Like no other time in history, we've got information literally at our fingertips, and yet, we are dealing with unprecedented, escalating statistics that prove my point.

In America alone, eight out of ten people admit to struggling with moderate to high levels of stress, and one in twelve deal with mild to moderate depression, of which 50 percent are experiencing difficulty in functioning at work and in day to day life. The suicide rate has increased 24 percent in the last ten years, the divorce rate is at 50 percent, over seventy million adults are obese, ninety-nine million are overweight, and over five hundred thousand people are homeless every night.

Granted, many factors are at play here, and my objective is not to itemize those reasons or point fingers but to bring to light that we are dealing with big issues and real numbers that aren't getting better. Yet our access to resources, options, solutions, and real answers has never been higher. The bottom line is we have more information than we even know what to do with, so information in and of itself is not the answer. If it were just as easy as Googling an answer, those statistics wouldn't be what they are. If you Google "how to lose weight," you can find thousands of legitimate answers. If you Google "how do you have more joy in your life," you can find pages upon pages of different ideas.

We know, but we don't *know.*

We comprehend at a head level, but we haven't taken it to *heart level.*

We hear, but we don't *believe.*

So how does one cross the line from knowing to *knowing?* From head to *heart?* From hearing to *believing?* The answer is action. We don't just think our way to acting; *we act our way to thinking.*

Action is the answer. And just as before, not any kind of action but *wholehearted action.*

What do I mean by wholehearted action?

Let's look back and reference what it means to live wholehearted in our action: it means going *all* in. It means doing things in entirety and completeness. It's action that is undivided, unbroken, undamaged, and aligned!

And let's face it, it's hard.

We like the *idea* of action more than we like taking action.

We like the *idea* of faith more than faith itself.

We like the *idea* of our dreams more than the actual work it takes to manifest them.

We like having information at our beck and call, but actually doing something about it, well, that's a different story. That's hard.

But truth be told, *everything* you're wanting is found in the work you're avoiding. That's where all the magic happens! That's where you find out a lot about you. It reveals you to you. You see what you're made of. You see where you've got work to do. You wake up to what you're capable of. Plus, you begin to see what God's capable of. Too many times, we play small, don't take risks, don't step out, and then wonder why we don't see miracles. We wonder why we don't see the "impossible" become possible. My question to you is this, are you creating "… but God" moments?

There was no way, *but God …*

I did all I could do, *but God …*

I couldn't find the answer, *but God …*

I didn't know the next step, *but God …*

But God moments introduce the amazing intervention and power of God in our lives. It captures the nature of who God is, the Dream Maker. This type of revelation sets you free.

Freedom isn't about being able to do what you want to do. Freedom is about doing what's right for you. It's about alignment with yourself and God. Freedom is about doing what God put in you to do. When you do this, you exchange your burden for His, "For my yoke is easy and my burden is light" (Matthew 11:30).

Let me ask you this, if you are free, completely free—free to have your dreams, free to pursue your dreams, free to obtain your dreams—what would you do today? What would you do this week? What would you do this month? Yes, it's going to take work. Yes, it's going to take commitment. Yes, it's going to take consistency and persistence, but if you're free to choose and you're in alignment with yourself and God, you no longer have all that unnecessary baggage dragging along behind you. "But Julia, you don't understand. I need accountability, or I won't do it." Exactly! That's my point *exactly*. That's called laziness. That's called apathy. That's called the opposite of wholehearted action. That's called misalignment. That's called not using your limitless vision and conviction, and you know better than that. You *know* more than that and the person you should be most accountable to is you. If you struggle with accountability, maybe instead of continuing to put off tomorrow what you could do today or putting on someone else what you can do for yourself, start working your own muscle of *self*-accountability. *You* hold yourself accountable the way that you would want someone else to. Give yourself the kind of tough love you want from someone else because that person will come and go, but you are with you forever.

Here's what I've come to learn, after being a straight-A student all my life; running my own business at the age of twenty-one; coaching hundreds and hundreds of entrepreneurs on strategic planning, and setting goals, deadlines, and dates to accomplish things: the best thing you can do for yourself as it pertains to taking massive action is to consider and reconsider your limitless vision and your conviction in light of your dreams. Remember, it's your *can't not.* Your "I don't know how I'll live with myself if I don't do it." Your God-ordained, purposed mission statement for your life. No midterm final, strategic plan, or deadline ever compares with the fire a true conviction has. When do I want to "live free" (my conviction)? Every day. When do I want to see a world where we create uninhibitedly (my limitless vision)? Right now. Right here. So what does my daily and weekly agenda look like? Anything in support of that cause.

You're going to take your limitless vision and conviction, align it with your dreams, and you're going to *do* something about it. Prove to yourself that it matters not in just word but in deed. Prove that it matters more than the fear. Prove that it matters more than the doubt. Prove that it matters more than what someone else might think. Prove that it matters more than the potential failure and trial and error along the way. PROVE IT! But don't just prove it to me, prove it to yourself. Every. Single. Day.

If you have to side hustle to make it happen, do that.

If you have to quit your job to make it happen, do that.

If you have to stay up late, get up early, do that.

If you have to ask for help, get a shorter to-do list, learn something you don't yet know, do that.

If you have to eat differently, make a few more calls, take a few more classes, practice a few more times, do that.

Do it because it gets you one step closer with each step you take. Do it because it honors your soul. Do it because it defies the fear and stands against everything you protest. Do it because you were born to.

And as you do, watch your life transform. Watch the "impossible" turn possible. Watch as God meets you in those *but God* moments. Watch as you no longer sit on the sidelines of life but rather get in the game. Watch as you move through ups and downs, good days and hard days, overcoming obstacles, hard conversations, and learn about all the stuff you didn't once know. Watch as you feel *every* emotion. Watch as you laugh, cry, feel fear, anger, peace, love, and pure joy. Watch all of it. It's called life, my friend. A life lived with your *whole* heart. Do it with ALL your heart. Do it with your limitless vision in mind. Do it with your conviction in mind. Do it because you can't not. Do it because God ordained, destined, and commissioned you to. Do it.

If you don't, if you choose to do nothing with your dreams, they will die with you. They will mean nothing to this world. No matter how real. No matter how big. No matter how beautiful your dreams are. You have to take what you know, and you have to make it real. The only way it will become real is if you take one step, and then another, and then another, and then, guess what? You don't stop!

By taking action, you will prove your fears, worry, and doubt to be mirages. Sure, your fears, worries, and doubts will seem bigger at first, but as soon as you move and reposition yourself, you will notice that your dreams are actually bigger; you were just at the wrong angle. Give your dreams more credit and reposition yourself on the other side of fear, worry, and doubt and see first-hand how much bigger your dreams (and God) really are.

By taking action, you no longer concern yourself with what other people think. It's a good thing your dreams aren't impacted by other people's opinions. You shouldn't be either. Your dreams aren't for the affection or approval of other people. Your dreams aren't caught up in people-pleasing, and as soon as you start to follow their lead, your need for approval will also fade away. It's no longer about concerning yourself with what other people think or say; it's about what your dreams say. It's about what God says.

By taking action, you will learn a lot! Many people shy away from taking massive action because they convince themselves they don't know enough. "I need to learn more," they say. Fair. Unless it's not. Sure, school and learning are great, but there is a fine line between learning and hiding. Learning in the classroom will only get you so far. Reading books will only teach you so much. Going back to school for the third time will only provide you with so much information, but remember that information is pointless IF we don't do something with it. Get out and play ball, and you will learn a ton more than just sitting in the classroom hearing lectures about it. Get in the car and drive, and you will learn more than reading a book about it. Get out and start building your business, and you will experience more than you could ever learn in school. Action will give you the tools you need exactly when you need them. Earn what you know.

By taking action, you will learn more about you. As mentioned, action will teach you about you! Action will show you first-hand what you're really made of. As you begin to move forward, stuff is going to come up, both good and bad. "What's inside the toothpaste" is bound to reveal itself. You will begin to see more clearly where your strengths are and where your weaknesses are. Action will show you what you're made of, what's going on at a heart level. It will reveal your capacity, and give you a much better understanding of what you have to do next in order to grow.

By taking action, you'll develop the confidence you're currently

waiting on. Part of the reason you don't feel confident today is twofold. Number one, like the levels of competency you learned in chapter 4, no one feels confident doing something they've never done before. It's the land of the consciously incompetent, and let's be honest, none of us like feeling consciously unskilled. Number two, confidence isn't built by just being good at something. Confidence is built by learning to trust yourself. People who trust themselves the most have the most amount of confidence. If you struggle with confidence, it's highly likely that it's not a confidence issue; it's a trust issue. Do you trust you? Are you keeping the promises you make to yourself? The more you trust yourself, the more risks you're able to take, and the more consciously incompetent zones you're able to step into because even though you don't feel good at something or you might fail, you can at least count on *you*. *You* have your own back. *You* trust *you*. By taking action toward the things that are most important to you, not only are you leveling up in your competency and skill, but you are also learning to trust yourself even more, which builds your confidence. If you want more confidence, make more promises to yourself that you're actually going to keep because you will always know. When you say, "I'm going to get up and go to the gym three times this week," you do it. You keep the promise to yourself. When you say, "I am going to call ten people this week who can help me get this project rolling," you do it because you keep the promises you make to yourself, no matter how big or how small. You do that enough times, over enough days, and slowly but surely, you build up the confidence necessary to sustain it.

By taking action, you'll kill the façade of perfection. Action is an exploration game, not a perfection game. Whew! Doesn't that just set you free to live your life! Pursuing your dreams is messy—as is life. Taking action is not as much about being right or wrong as we might think. It is not a game for perfectionists. Action is an exploration game. It's about figuring things out as you go. It's trusting that you will find the answer as you need to. It's about doing your part and letting God do the rest. It's about getting your hands dirty and not letting failures mean anything more than "try something else." This allows you to take action before you're ready or before you're well versed before all the T's are crossed and I's are dotted. Allow your action to show you the way, and allow God to direct your steps, one step at a time. When you do this, you'll begin to enjoy the process even more because you're not so stressed about being right or wrong, and you'll have fun exploring, just as a child would. We make life so much harder than it needs to be. We build in unnecessary pressures, and a stressed person makes for a stressed journey, but a faith-filled person makes for a faith-filled journey. This should be fun, otherwise, what's the point?!

By taking action, you get present in the here and now. From the smallest steps to the biggest steps, action toward your dreams is beautiful because it will lead you out of the addiction to the past and free you from the anxiety of the future. It needs you completely present in the *here* and *now*. I always find it funny that one of the things I hear people say the most is they want to "live present." They want to be more present in their lives, more present at their work, more present to their families, and to the moments that are unfolding before them. Then they get clear and begin to realize how much control they *don't* have and how much of life they *cannot* predict, and, suddenly, those same people resent it. They freak out because they want the whole plan. They want to know how the story ends. They want to control their future. Be careful what you wish for. Your dreams will require you to get present by causing you to live in the here and now. They will require you to learn how to trust God's provision for your life because you don't receive the whole plan mapped out with a pretty red bow. Often, all you get is the next step. The Bible says, "Give us *today* our *daily* bread" (Matthew 6:11 [emphasis mine]). You won't know how next quarter or next month is going to pan out. Heck, you may only get insights into today. That is okay. Get comfortable asking yourself: What's the *one* next step? One thing leads to the next, which leads to the next, which, yes, leads to the next. Don't miss the signs. Don't miss the signals. Just get present in the here and now.

DREAM—I Dare You

Action has a way of killing procrastination fast. People who procrastinate have a skewed perspective of time, and they often don't value it. It seems trite to say, but none of us are guaranteed tomorrow. All of us only get one life to live. Waiting until tomorrow or putting it off for another day begins to negate the fact that your life is so very precious, and you are not guaranteed anything more than this present moment and the choices you make today. You only get twenty-four hours each day. With every hour that goes by, you are either moving toward your dreams or moving away from them. You are either investing in your limiting belief or your limitless vision. You are either investing in fear or faith. Consider each hour and use them all to stack your cards toward the fulfillment of your dreams. The rest can wait. Sure, with action you're going to fail, make mistakes, and you are going to learn fast, but you will never look back and wish you had tried because you will live your life *trying*. Live to try. Live your life giving it a shot! You won't know until you go, and if you won't know until you go, then the best thing you could do is go. Now. Don't think about it; just go! Just do it. No more delaying, waiting, making excuses, or saying "I'll do it tomorrow." The time to pursue your dreams is always now. When you find yourself wondering, "When is a good time to pursue my dreams?" just refer back to this sentence: *The time to pursue your dreams is always now.*

It's time!

It's Time For Action

With all of that being said, let's get a bit more granular with this. Tomorrow you wake up, and it's time to move toward your dreams; how do you do that? How do you line out your action steps? How do you ensure you are moving toward your dreams in the midst of competing commitments? The answer is in your daily check-ins.

Let's just say this, there will always be competing noise *disguised* as commitments, so it's important that you learn to check in on your dreams every day. The point of a daily check-in is to make sure your dreams are

226

louder than everything else on that list. If we're not careful, one day turns into the next, and slowly but surely, everything else that has been vying for your attention begins to win. Put your dreams on your list first. Otherwise, who else will? It's never that we don't have enough time. We all have exactly the same amount of time. We all have twenty-four hours given to us each day, which tells me that if other people are pursuing and accomplishing their dreams, you can too; you may just need to reprioritize.

That means, every day, you are literally going to *check-in* with yourself to ensure your thoughts and dreams align with your action. Here's what this check-in might look like:

1. Renew your mind! You need to ensure that your head is in alignment with your heart. No doubt about it, you're head is going to get off course and it's going to be your job to ensure that it's in alignment with where you're heart is at. When renewing your mind, you are going to consciously remind yourself of all Biblical principles that support you and your life's mission. You are going to remind yourself that you are born to dream and to chase every dream you can imagine. You are going to remind yourself that the God of this Universe has your back. You are going to remind yourself that *you* have your back. You are going to remind yourself of your limitless vision, your conviction, your protest, and every single dream that you have on the inside of yourself. You are going to take your thoughts captive first because your head just has this funny way of forgetting. This first step is non-negotiable!

2. Visualize your dreams. You are going to embody them, become them, and saturate yourself in them. You are going to familiarize yourself with the things that God put in you to do! You're not going to see it in the world around you until you can take the time to see it within you.

3. Act like It. You are going to bring your future into today by *acting as though it exists* now. Today. Don't wait for "when you get there" to live with vital energy or to impact people with greater love and care, do it now! Don't wait to act like the person who has lost thirty pounds or the author who has published handfuls of books; begin to act like that person *today*. Right now.

Don't wait for the accomplishment of that dream to suddenly become that person. Instead, practice being that person right now, in this moment! So yes, losing thirty pounds will aid you in living with more energy, but what would it look like today, in this moment, to begin living like it? You'd ask yourself, what would the thirty-pound lighter version of me say? What would God say? Let's say you dream of being wealthy and you want to do great things with your money. Sure, making more money would help you bless more people, but who says they need your money? Or who says a quarter won't go a long way? And even so, what would the wealthier you say to the you of today? What would the wealthy you do with the resources you have now? Do you see what I'm saying? This allows you to start pulling your future into your present moment. You begin to develop the mindset and the habits of becoming that person *today*, not just when it happens. By visualizing and then embodying that dream now, you start to become it, and you start making decisions in alignment with it. Once you do this, I want you to consider any of the following prompting questions to get you moving (because the value of your question determines the value of your answer):

What could I do today that would move my dream forward?

What would I do this week, this month?

What do I need to learn to get going?

Who do I need to talk to?

If I wasn't afraid, what would I do right now?

If it was safe for me to know, what would I need to know?

Who could I call or ask for help?

Who is already doing something like this that I could learn from?

What will be the hardest parts about accomplishing this dream, and how can I strengthen myself to be prepared?

What will it take to be successful?

What does the Bible say about this?

Answers will start to look like this:
- Call three people in the industry to learn more.
- Research _____ to have a better understanding.
- Go see a nutritionist to give me a better starting point.
- Get into the gym two times this week.
- Hire a personal trainer.
- Start writing. Write one chapter.
- Quit my job.
- Put in five offers.
- Create the website.
- Identify who or what I need most.
- Increase sales by 10 percent by doing social media marketing consistently.
- Forgive seventy times seven times.

Right now, consider your dreams and tell me the first five to ten things you can do to start moving toward those dreams *today*. Ready, go. Don't wait, don't hesitate, don't overthink it, write those things down now:

_____

_____

_____

_____

_____

When doubt, fear, worry, anxiety, and your limiting beliefs pop up, because they will, don't try to ignore them. Don't fool yourself into believing that you shouldn't be feeling or thinking those things (you are human). Instead, acknowledge what you're feeling, understand why (because you're stepping into an unfamiliar heaven and the mind chatter is only freaking out), and then free it by giving it something else to focus on. Take one action item from the above list and do it. And when you're done with that one thing, do the next thing.

It helps if you can identify these five to ten things before an unclear, freak-out moment occurs, so when that moment does occur, you have something you can land on. It's easy to get overwhelmed with the "100 things" you have to do; it's easy to get overwhelmed by the lack of money, resources, or support; it's easy to get overwhelmed by the lack of clarity. So in those moments, I want you to reference the list of five to ten things that you _can_ do. Do them. And then, don't stop.

So there you have it!

You've got a Limitless Vision.

You've got a Conviction.

You've got a Protest.

You've got Dreams.

And now you've got a course of action!

You, my friend, have got your life back! The light within you is shining ever so brightly, which is a good thing because the world around you needs the light within you. The world needs who you are created to be. The world needs your dreams. It's time to be bold as lions!

Now, go live. Alive. Awake. Go live like a dreamer—because, guess what? You are.

Make sure your DREAMS are louder than everything else on your to do list. You manifest your DREAMS for tomorrow by acting like it today.

ABOUT JULIA GENTRY

BY THE AGE OF TWENTY-THREE, Julia built a successful company in real estate that bought and sold millions of dollars' worth of investment property only to end up $100,000 in debt. She then rebuilt her career as a business coach, advising hundreds of entrepreneurs on how to build a successful business. She bought the house and nice cars, had a few babies, and obtained "the American dream" only to realize it wasn't her dream. Every night as she crawled  into bed, she had this nagging question in the back of her mind: IS THERE SOMETHING MORE?

Then, she had a **"midlife awakening."**

Thankfully, she identified the answer to that question (YES), and she has become a "wake-up call" that the people of the world didn't know they always needed!

As a dreamer, author, business owner, Jesus follower, passionate wife, wild mom of four, and founder of The Dream Factory and Co., she provides a fresh, bold approach to creating greater alignment in life and encourages a more awakened way to live. She is on a mission to create a massive wake-up call that ignites people, outside the walls of the church, to be the light in the dark, the salt of the earth, and to be bold as lions in their faith, family, career, and community.

Currently, we don't know where Julia lives or what she's doing next, but you can be sure it's somewhere between brilliant and insane.

Follow her journey at TheDreamFactoryandCo.com.

DREAMER'S RESOURCES

IF YOU'RE LOOKING TO GROW and you want to amplify what you just learned in this book or you simply want to get involved in a community of dreamers, please be sure to check out all our resources!

DREAM: Gather

This book will light a fire within you, which is why we have created **DREAM: Gather** which is designed specifically for groups of people who are looking to expand or enhance their connections with people and just want deeper, more meaningful conversations. This is perfect for book clubs, small groups, church groups, MOPS groups, and even small businesses. We provide you with everything you need to get your group up and running, and each group member receives a book, the workbook, videos and downloads, and two months of free membership in our online community DREAM: Together. If you are interested in starting or joining a group, contact dream@thedreamfactoryandco.com.

DREAM: Together

Our online membership site has been created for dreamers to connect and collaborate, learn and grow, to be encouraged and challenged as they grow on their journey. This membership site is incredible because all of our offerings are first LIVE so you can join in and interact with our team as well as other dreamers all across the country in our weekly and monthly sessions. We provide content and coaching for mental and emotional health/wellbeing, growth in business, support for moms, evening prayer, and even a kids corner for children to get involved! To learn more, go to TheDreamFactoryandCo. com/dreamtogether.

DREAM: Now

We offer an online, seven-week, group coaching course called **DREAM: Now** that is led by one of our trained growth coaches. This course is designed to walk you through the entire book, week by week, step by step, in a coaching experience that takes your dream work to a whole new level! We start a new "hub" every month. Gain access to our FREE introduction video or get involved today at TheDreamFactoryandCo.com/dreamnow.

One on One Coaching

This is a 6-12 month private coaching program designed for business owners, leadership teams, or anyone who wants to go further and faster in a much more hands-on approach. There is no one-size-fits all dream which means there is no one-right-way to doing things. Our coaches are trained to support you in creating a personalized roadmap from where you are to where you want to be in perfect alignment with who you are, where you are, and what you want most. This level of growth coaching demands a lot but is incredible in its results. Apply today at TheDreamFactoryandCo.com/coaching

ALL of these programs are designed to amplify the learned concepts within this book and create a more experiential understanding so all of it comes alive to you in your life! No matter which option you choose, we are here to help you destroy your limiting beliefs, create a solid vision for your life, and clarify the dreams that God has put within you so you can stop avoiding the things that you want most and instead live unapologetically and bold as lions in your faith, family, career, and community!

Dreamer, we're waiting for you…

A PRAYER OF SALVATION

THE GREATEST DAY IN YOUR LIFE will be the day that you realize there is a God that holds the entire universe in His hands, and not only does He hold the entire universe, He holds *you* in His hands. He loves you and He *chose* you before the creation of time.

The next greatest day is the day that you choose Him in return.

If you've read this book and God has become alive to you in a whole new way, a God that is so much bigger and more real than anything this world could ever offer, and you want to accept Him into your life, we would be honored to lead you in a prayer of surrender. The Bible says, "Everyone who calls on the name of the Lord will be saved" (Romans 10:13). If this speaks to you and you want to know this God, pray with us…

Dear God. I humbly bow before you today and I say thank you. Thank you for making yourself real to me. Thank you for this moment. I surrender to you. I surrender my desires, my hopes, my dreams, my life. I believe that Jesus was born without sin, that he died on a cross for my sins, and that he rose three days later. I believe in your salvation and the eternal life you offer me because of this sacrifice that was made for me. I repent of all my ways and all my wayward thinking and I invite your son, Jesus Christ, into my heart. Be my Lord. Today, I ask for new life. I ask for the life that only you, through Jesus and the power of the Holy Spirit, can provide. Thank you for your forgiveness, your majesty, and for all that you do. In Jesus' name, Amen.

If you prayed this prayer, we encourage you to not do this alone. Though this prayer is absolutely a life-changing prayer, it is just the beginning of a life-long process. A process that really is the best thing you could ever do and, it's hard. Just as dreamers shouldn't dream alone, believers shouldn't believe alone. Please be sure to become involved with a church near you, to learn and grow, and to develop your faith into one that moves mountains. We also encourage you to get a Bible to support you in your journey. Hebrews says, "For the word of God is alive and active" (Hebrews 4:12). If you do not yet have your own Bible, we would love to be a part of this step. Please email us at dream@thedreamfactoryandco.com and we will personally send you a life-changing gift of your very own Bible. Welcome home!

Made in USA - Kendallville, IN
93606_9781735785905
09.16.2023 1347